HEROES
OF THE FAITH

British Library Cataloguing in Publication Data

A catalogue record for this book is available from the British Library

ISBN: 978-1-912326-18-1

Cover and title page illustrations by Jennie Carew.
Illustrations © 2022 Philo Trust. Used by permission.

Design Management by Jeni Child
jenichil@hotmail.com

Print Management by Verité CM Ltd
www.veritecm.com

Printed in the UK

HEROES
OF THE FAITH

CONTENTS

Acknowledgements

Many people have played a significant part in compiling and producing *Heroes of the Faith*.

I would like to thank my researcher Dr Chris Walley – thank you, Chris, for meticulously checking that all the facts and details are correct and for finding such amazing heroes of the faith.

Special thanks to my wife Killy for her sage advice. She is my devoted encourager and my most trusted critic. Our partnership in marriage and ministry makes every book hers too.

Huge thanks to my colleague Sam Rennie, our production manager – you have excelled in managing and bringing together the many details to create a book we can be proud of. Thank you also to my colleague Jamie Bennett for numerous hours spent in picture research, and to our other colleagues Val Aballay, Dave Reynolds, Emily Clode, Steve Murrill and Genevieve Schroeder for numerous 'what do you think of this' meetings!

Our grateful thanks to Jeni Child, our designer, picture researcher and illustrator – you have created a beautiful book that is appealing and easy to read.

Thank you to Louise Stenhouse, our proofreader – we so appreciate you reading and re-reading the manuscript.

And many thanks to Chris and Cathy Powell who manage our publishing and printing – you have excelled.

And thanks be to our Lord and Saviour Jesus Christ – you 'ransomed, healed, restored and forgave' our fifty heroes so they could be channels of your love and grace to others.

PREFACE

When I first came to faith in Christ as a student in 1975 I read numerous biographies and was deeply impacted and inspired. Many of the people from those biographies are featured in these pages.

For two thousand years billions of people have followed Jesus Christ. This volume of fifty men and women – scientists, doctors, scholars, writers, reformers, preachers, missionaries, abolitionists and evangelists – portrays stories of faith, love, generosity, sacrifice and perseverance.

My prayer and hope is that these portraits of Christian men and women who changed their world in their own significant way will give you a faith-lift and inspire you to do what you can, with what you have, wherever you are.

These fifty heroes of the faith are just a few of the 'cloud of witnesses' recorded in Hebrews.

> *Therefore, since we are surrounded by so great a cloud of witnesses, let us also lay aside every weight, and sin which clings so closely, and let us run with endurance the race that is set before us, looking to Jesus, the founder and perfecter of our faith, who for the joy that was set before him endured the cross, despising the shame, and is seated at the right hand of the throne of God.* (Hebrews 12:1-2 ESV)

Amen. Let us 'run with endurance the race that is set before us'.

WILLIAM WILBERFORCE

One Christian hero who stands high is William Wilberforce (1759-1833). Although he is remembered mainly for leading the battle against slavery, he did an enormous amount of good in many other areas.

Wilberforce was born into a Yorkshire family and after going to Cambridge University, where he seems to have done as little in the way of studying as possible, he became an MP in 1780. He was to later admit that at this time he had no other ambition than to promote his own career.

In 1784 his life changed when he converted to the Christian faith. He took his new relationship with God so seriously that he considered becoming a clergyman, but accepted advice to stay in politics. He soon became involved with other Christians who were determined to work out their faith in changing society for the better. For many of them the pressing issue of the time was the abomination of slavery and the evil trade associated with it. Wilberforce joined them and, gifted with eloquence, he became the champion of the anti-slavery cause and made it his life's mission. Although bitterly opposed by those

Wilberforce House, the birthplace of William Wilberforce.

who had interests in what was a very profitable business, Wilberforce persistently introduced Bills from 1789 onwards to abolish first the slave trade and then slavery itself. Despite defeat after defeat he persisted until finally, in 1833, just three days before his death, the British government passed the Bill to abolish slavery. His lifelong battle had been victorious.

Beyond the Abolition of Slavery

Wilberforce was also involved in many other social issues: he campaigned on behalf of single mothers, orphans, Sunday schools, juvenile delinquents and children employed as chimney sweeps. He helped set up many organisations such as the Church Missionary Society and the British and Foreign Bible Society, and was a founder member of one of the first charities against animal cruelty, known today as the RSPCA. Although it has what is now an unfashionable title, his Society for the Suppression of Vice stood against many of the social evils of his day – and, sadly, ours – drunkenness, corruption, prostitution and animal cruelty.

The House of Commons in 1808.

In these days, when every figure of the past is scrutinised by whatever standards are currently held, there are those who might find fault with Wilberforce. He was as much a man of his time as we are of ours, and on many social issues was very conservative. Yet, as he would be the first to agree, the ultimate issue is not how any of us measure against the fluctuating and ever-changing standards

Anti-slavery seal for the English Committee for the Abolition of the Slave Trade.

that our culture creates, but how we measure up against those of God. Indeed, if we are to condemn, we should remember that to judge is to be judged. If we point a finger in accusation it means three fingers point back at us. After all, it is not as though we live in a time of no evils or injustices. Were he alive today, I think Wilberforce would be a busy man.

Let me suggest five things that challenge me about William Wilberforce.

- First, *he applied his faith*. As many Christians have done, before and since, he could easily have separated his spiritual life from his daily work. He didn't. With Wilberforce there was a wonderful harmony between what he believed and what he sought to achieve.

- Second, *he served in costly leadership*. A small, frail man with poor health, Wilberforce willingly took on a role that he knew would make him a target. We may view him as little short of a saint today but for many of his contemporaries he was a man of dangerous ideas who deserved to be criticised and obstructed. He paid the price for leadership.

- Third, *he had determination*. Wilberforce persisted in his battle against slavery, not just for months or years, but for decades. He realised his calling and he stuck with it. His was truly a 'purpose-driven life'.

- Fourth, *he had wisdom*. Wilberforce was a strategic thinker, sought the support of others and built friendships and alliances from as wide a circle as possible.

The Palace of Westminster, London, informally known as the Houses of Parliament.

- Fifth, **he guarded his spiritual life**. With all his involvements and activities, Wilberforce could easily have had his faith crushed under the weight of his duties and responsibilities. Yet he knew that only God could be the source of the strength he needed. To the very end of his life he remained permanently dependent on the grace of God.

William Wilberforce was an example of a true conversion to Christ. Today, some are cynical of an individual 'becoming converted' or being 'born again'. If any sort of change to faith is talked about, it's that of a gradual process or some sort of 'spiritual journey'. The unarguable reality with Wilberforce is that he did undergo a dramatic transforming conversion. He reminds us that conversions do happen, and that they can have remarkable effects.

Finally, given that Wilberforce was already a Member of Parliament when he converted to the Christian faith, it inspires me to pray for the same thing to happen to today's politicians.

The bookplate of William Wilberforce.

JOSEPHINE BUTLER

Josephine Butler (1828–1906) was one of the most important Englishwomen of the nineteenth century.

She worked tirelessly for decades trying to rescue prostitutes and prevent women being trafficked into prostitution and, in doing so, exposed a dreadful business that many people – especially men – would have preferred to remain hidden. Unfortunately, she paid the price: those who tackle an unmentionable evil often become unmentionable themselves.

A Personal and Cultural Portrait

Josephine was born into an upper-middle-class Christian family who were very interested in social reform and who treated her education with a seriousness rare at that time. In her teenage years Josephine's childhood faith was deepened through a spiritual experience that gave her a profound love for Christ. She married a man who not only loved her deeply but shared her faith and was prepared to treat her as an equal. Just when a life of quiet respectability seemed guaranteed, tragedy struck with the death of a daughter in 1863, and Josephine – always sensitive to injustice – began to occupy herself in charity work, visiting workhouses and rescuing prostitutes from the streets.

A combination of social and economic factors had meant that prostitution was widespread in Victorian Britain. It was covered by weak laws and policed with a harsh insensitivity. Unpleasant as it is to mention, prostitutes were treated as villains rather than victims, frequently abused – there are appalling references to 'padded rooms' in brothels – and in an age when there was no treatment for sexual diseases, virgins were much prized. Matters were made worse by Victorian sensitivities which meant that the injustices and cruelties were hidden because 'decent' people would not mention or investigate them.

Thinking Strategically

Josephine adopted a double strategy. She simply befriended prostitutes, speaking to them of Jesus and, where possible, offered them a way out. Some she housed in her own home, others in hostels. Yet she also 'went public' and, gifted with intelligence, charm and good looks, began public meetings to take her campaign against prostitution and female injustice to the nation. It took courage as she was subjected to repeated verbal and sometimes physical attacks. For a woman to speak publicly was unusual in the Victorian era and for one to speak on sexual matters was felt to be an outrage.

A Harlot's Progress, a series of paintings and engravings that show the story of a young woman who arrives in London from the countryside and becomes a prostitute.

Despite frequent ill-health Josephine tirelessly travelled backwards and forwards across the country speaking everywhere she was allowed to. She soon made strategic friends and, as the years passed, saw bad laws repealed and good laws introduced. In the 1880s she began a campaign against child prostitution which resulted in the age of consent being raised from thirteen to sixteen, a move which made the prosecution of the men involved possible.

St Gregory's Church, Kirknewton, the final resting place of Josephine Butler.

Josephine's passion extended beyond the injustices of prostitution to every area in which women were badly treated. She was a prime mover in demanding that women's education be taken seriously and an early advocate for a woman's right to vote. Her interests and enthusiasm took her to the Continent where she encouraged action there against prostitution and other injustices. It is fascinating to note that Josephine campaigned vigorously against a system by which the British Army in India obtained large numbers of local prostitutes in order to protect the health of its soldiers.

Josephine was in every way a remarkable woman and her life and actions pose all sorts of challenges to us today. There are the obvious things: her commitment, her sacrifice, her courage and her passion. There is also, of course, her relevance: a century and a half later such things as child abuse, people trafficking, prostitution and the sexual mistreatment of women have not gone away.

Yet there are many other aspects to her life. Let me list five that I find fascinating.

- First, **Josephine was a woman of faith**. Josephine was driven by a living faith in Jesus in which daily prayer and Bible study were essential. One of her famous sayings was, 'God and one woman make a majority.'

Left: Map Descriptive of London Poverty by Charles Booth, 1898-1899.

It appears from the Handbills issued by MR. CHILDERS this morning, that

HE IS AFRAID TO MEET US,

And answer our questions on the Contagious Diseases Acts.

THEREFORE

MRS. BUTLER

REQUESTS THE

WOMEN OF PONTEFRACT

TO MEET HER AT THE

LARGE ROOM, IN SOUTHGATE,

(USED BY MR. JOHNSON AS A SPINNING ROOM),

THIS EVENING AT SEVEN O'CLOCK.

MRS. BUTLER will shew that the Bill of which MR. CHILDERS says he is now a supporter, while pretending to Repeal the "Contagious Diseases Acts" is an extension of their principle to the whole country. MRS. BUTLER will shew that MR. CHILDERS belongs to a Government which has extended these Acts not only to this Country but to the Colonies and Dependencies of the British Empire.

JOSEPHINE E. BUTLER, Hon. Sec. of the Ladies' National Association.

Handbill issued by Josephine Butler prior to a talk during the 1872 Pontefract by-election.

- Second, *Josephine was a woman of grace*. While many Victorian Christians abhorred the horrors of prostitution, they took a cold and condemning approach that ended up punishing the women involved. Josephine shunned judgement and instead showed friendship and love for those at the heart of this evil trade. Ultimately her battle was not against prostitution as a system but for prostitutes as people.

- Third, *Josephine didn't close her eyes*. While only a small minority of the population may have actually used prostitutes in the nineteenth century, the vast majority chose simply to look away. After all, prostitution was a business that was conducted largely at night, behind closed doors and which generally involved 'girls of the lower classes'. Josephine realised that in the face of evil, it's not enough simply to turn your face away. She acted.

- Fourth, *Josephine was prepared to break the rules of society*. She chose to do what society said she mustn't do. In doing so she was, of course, following the pattern of Jesus who shocked his contemporaries with his friendship for those who were considered sinners.

- Finally, *Josephine recognised the limits of the law*. Yes, she was a great social reformer, but she was under no illusions that morality could save society or individuals. Josephine's great hope was the transformation of lives through an encounter with Jesus.

In the current climate there are a lot of empty plinths where statues have been removed. A very suitable replacement would be one of Josephine Butler. I suspect, however, that had you asked her whether she wanted to be commemorated in some iron or bronze figure, she would have said that her best memorial was the continuation of her work. I'd agree.

BILLY BRAY

One of my heroes is the Cornish evangelist Billy Bray. I read his biography soon after becoming a Christian and was hugely impacted and inspired.

Billy was born in 1794 in Cornwall. Born in poverty and barely educated, Billy became a tin miner. Despite growing up amongst a Christian faith, he soon began living a life filled with drunkenness and violence. He married a woman who had been a keen Methodist but who had let her faith lapse. Nevertheless, his wife's memory of a happy former life challenged Billy and in 1823 he became desperately aware that he needed to 'begin again'. He pursued God, praying, reading the Bible and Wesley's hymns for days before eventually finding peace through Christ, and not long afterwards his wife returned to her faith.

Billy's conversion was radical and profound and a sense of wondrous deliverance never left him. In the next four decades, Billy's life was marked with an extraordinary and exuberant joy that he continually expressed in spontaneous jumping, dancing and shouting, whether at work down the mine or in preaching. He lived simply and served his needy community. Billy gave away money without any concern for how it was to be replaced, raised orphans and built chapels.

The parish church of Saint Michael and All Angels in Baldhu where Billy Bray is buried.

The heart of the
Cornish tin-mining
district, looking
from Dolcoath Mine
towards Redruth
c. 1890.

Billy continued working in the mine, rejoicing in his labours and bringing many of his workmates to faith. Increasingly, however, he preached both in chapels and outdoors, becoming a household name across Cornwall. He was passionate and witty and his preaching drew the crowds. Many people came simply for the spectacle of seeing him, only to return home converted.

Two quotes can summarise Billy the man. The first is a phrase he frequently used about praying: 'I must talk to Father about that.' The second is a defence of his exuberance: 'Well, I dance sometimes. Why shouldn't I dance as well as David? David, you say, was a king; well, bless the Lord! I am a King's Son! I have as good a right to dance as David had.' Taken together, that sense of being both a child of God the Father and an heir to the King of kings explains much about him.

Billy Bray died in 1868, and the final word on his lips was '*Glory*!'

I find four things that speak to me about Billy Bray.

• First, *I'm challenged by Billy's joy*. Life was tough in the mining communities of early nineteenth-century Cornwall and Billy was always a poor man living amidst bitter poverty. Yet every mention of him speaks of his extraordinary joy, happiness and cheerfulness. He did indeed rejoice in his salvation. We who live easier, richer lives could benefit from his depth of unshakeable joy.

17

- Second, *I'm challenged by Billy's witness*. For many Christians, sharing the faith is something that has to be encouraged. There was nothing of that with Billy Bray: he was a man who simply couldn't help telling other people about Jesus. The gospel bubbled naturally out of him. May it do so with us!

- Third, *I'm challenged by Billy's simplicity*. Literacy and learning are good and I'm all in favour of theological colleges. Yet, in thinking about Billy Bray, I can't help but wonder if we have not paid too high a price for the pursuit of academia. Billy preached the simple gospel: because Jesus died for us, we should put our trust in him. It served him well in his day; I see no reason why it shouldn't serve us as well in ours.

- Fourth, *I'm challenged by Billy's authenticity*. I think it was the secret to much of his fruitfulness. Authenticity attracts and encourages trust.

Billy Bray was a personality of a particular time and place: a product of a culture as long gone as the tin mines that created it. One little uncomfortable fact opposes this view: those features that are challenging about Billy are seen everywhere in the pages of the New Testament, not least in the Book of Acts. The thought grips me that maybe Billy Bray was not so peculiar after all. Perhaps, and it's a troubling thought, it's not Billy who is the oddity but us.

A disused Cornish tin mine today.

HARRIET TUBMAN

I recently watched the movie Harriet *based on the true story of Harriet Tubman. I was inspired and, having since researched her, Harriet has now become one of my Christian heroes.*

Harriet was born into slavery in Maryland as Araminta Ross; she later changed her name to Harriet and took the Tubman from her husband. It is typical of Harriet's lowly status as a black slave that no one recorded the actual date of her birth in 1822. Like most slaves, Harriet received no education and was to remain illiterate all her life. She began work at the age of five as a housemaid and soon suffered all the brutalities of slavery: starvation, whippings, beatings and a particularly severe head injury that left her with lifelong problems. Yet amid this suffering, she was part of a dynamic church culture that gave her a firm faith in Christ. Harriet became a woman with a personal relationship with Christ; she sought his guidance and frequently had vivid visions.

Tubman on an American postage stamp.

Harriet grew up in tumultuous times. The United States was becoming deeply divided over slavery: while the southern states supported the practice, the northern ones banned it and granted slaves freedom. As a result, an increasing number of slaves in the southern states chose to flee northwards on the long and dangerous route to liberty and freedom. When Harriet was in her late twenties, she felt God urging her to flee. Guided by God and carefully avoiding the brutal slave catchers by using the organised network of guides and safe houses that came to be called the Underground Railroad, she fled to Pennsylvania. She was later to describe her feelings on crossing the boundary:

'When I found I had crossed that line, I looked at my hands to see if, now I was free, I was the same person. There was such a glory over everything; the sun came like gold through the trees, and over the fields, and I felt like I was in heaven.' Then, suddenly aware that she had to survive on her own, she prayed, 'Oh, dear Lord, I ain't got no friend but you. Come to my help, Lord, for I'm in trouble!'

At liberty, Harriet decided to rescue those she had left behind. So for eleven years she made dangerous journeys into Maryland, travelling through winter nights and hiding from slave hunters and

Workers managed a network of informants benefiting African Americans, free and enslaved.

Bestpitch Ferry Bridge. Part of the Harriet Tubman Underground Railroad Byway.

their dogs. She brought out family, friends and strangers through the Underground Railroad. She made nineteen expeditions south, escorting over 300 slaves to freedom. Among her own people she acquired the nickname of 'Moses' because of her role in bringing them to the 'Promised Land'. Her success and her ability to avoid capture became legendary. In part it was due to God guiding her and her courage, intelligence and determination. She was also helped because the increasingly troubled slave-owners came to believe they were dealing with a powerful man rather than a small black woman. Typically, Harriet attributed her success to the Lord's protection. Soon slave-owners posted wanted notices in which tens of thousands of dollars were offered for her, dead or alive.

Civil War

When in 1861 the tensions over slavery erupted into the Civil War, Harriet aligned herself with the Union Army of the North. With them she served as a laundress, cook and nurse but increasingly as a scout and spy. Familiar with the terrain and used to concealing herself within it, she located Confederate military positions and even guided raids into the South; on occasions wearing a uniform. In one remarkable raid she led an armed assault on a collection of plantations that successfully liberated 750 slaves. The idea that an

A woodcut of Tubman in her Civil War clothing.

HARRIET TUBMAN

Tubman (far left) with family and neighbours c. 1887.

American military operation might be led by a small, black, illiterate civilian woman might seem unbelievable, but truth is often stranger than fiction. In admiration, Harriet found herself called 'General Tubman'.

Harriet spent her latter years in good works with her church, campaigning for the fair treatment of African-Americans and promoting women's rights. She died on 10th March 1913 and was buried with military honours.

How does Harriet Tubman inspire and challenge me?

- First, **Harriet was full of faith.** She may have been illiterate but throughout her life she drew on rich resources of Christian faith and personal experience. God sustained her in war and peace and guided her.

- Second, **Harriet triumphed over extraordinary difficulties**. She was born into slavery and poverty, had no education and suffered much, including an almost crippling physical injury. Yet for all the little she had – or perhaps because of it – God was able to do great things through her.

- Third, **her faith in Christ gave her courage**. Harriet had the courage to carry out daring actions in perilous situations; she also had the courage to keep on battling on issues over years. Many of us could use a dose of that courage today.

Left: The Underground Railroad was a network of secret routes and safe houses used by slaves to escape to free states and Canada.

- Fourth, **she didn't get too comfortable**. When Harriet reached freedom, she could have stayed there. Instead she chose to make repeated return journeys to bring others to liberty. The idea that if you are saved you should save others is a good one.

- Finally, **she resisted hate**. The greatest danger in combating evil is that in the struggle you can become evil yourself. So many of Harriet's abolitionist contemporaries felt it was justifiable to kill slave-owners. She drew back from that: she shunned hatred and revenge. Her Christian faith gave her not just a resolve but also restraint. It's a good lesson.

Harriet Tubman was a woman who found herself at the heart of monumental issues. Despite being ill-equipped in almost every way, she leaned on God and was able to serve with remarkable success. We face very different battles than Harriet did, but we serve the same God. Let's hear God's voice like Harriet did and do his will with wisdom, patience and courage.

Tubman's home in Auburn, New York. Part of the Harriet Tubman National Historical Park.

JOHN BUNYAN

John Bunyan is one of the most influential Christians of all time. Although he wrote nearly sixty books, his influence rests on one: The Pilgrim's Progress. *It has sold more copies than any book other than the Bible and has helped countless numbers of people on the road to heaven.*

John Bunyan came from the most unpromising background and lived in troubled times. Born in 1628 to a poor Bedfordshire tinker (a man who made a living repairing pots and kettles), the young Bunyan had the minimum of schooling. At the age of sixteen he found himself on the Parliamentary side in the English Civil War, returning after three years to pick up his father's trade.

Bunyan had grown up without any Christian influence and as a young man was wild and lawless. Nevertheless, in the 1650s a variety of factors brought him to faith in Christ. It was not a straightforward conversion and a long, agonising struggle was to take place before Bunyan felt confident that he was indeed forgiven and saved.

The Pilgrim's Progress, 1678.

> *'May it please your Majesty, if I could possess that tinker's abilities to grip men's hearts, I would gladly give up all my learning.'*
>
> **JOHN OWEN**

Joining a Baptist church, Bunyan soon became widely recognised as one of the most powerful Puritan preachers of his day, attracting crowds of over a thousand. When King Charles II heard that John Owen, the leading Puritan theologian of his day and Vice Chancellor of Oxford University, had been to listen to Bunyan preach, the king asked him why he had been to hear a 'mere tinker'. The great man replied, 'May it please your Majesty, if I could possess that tinker's abilities to grip men's hearts, I would gladly give up all my learning.'

Jail Sentence

With the memory of the Civil War still fresh, the government of Charles II was anxious to suppress any form of dissent and England became an unwelcome place for those who, like Bunyan, were church leaders outside the national Anglican Church. In 1661 Bunyan found himself thrown in jail for his faith and ended up being imprisoned for twelve years. Bunyan had to live with the possibility that he might be sentenced to death, and his separation from his wife, family and church were a bitter pain to him. Locked away in jail, Bunyan began to write books. In 1672 he was released and pastored a Baptist church in Bedford until his death in 1688.

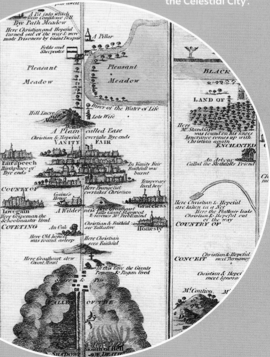

An allegorical 'roadmap' from an 1821 edition of *The Pilgrim's Progress* entitled 'The Road from the City of Destruction to the Celestial City'.

The birthplace of John Bunyan, a 15th-century timber-framed Moot Hall in the village of Elstow, Bedfordshire.

The Pilgrim's Progress, a work published in two parts in 1678 and 1684, is a remarkable book. At one level it is a novel of journeys in which various characters face enemies and dangers as they make their way to their destination of the Celestial City. Interwoven with this is insightful teaching on entering and living the Christian life. It is a skilfully told story that is creatively engaging.

As a preacher, pastor and writer Bunyan knew he was someone entrusted by God with a message to proclaim. How he delivered that message inspires me.

- First, Bunyan was **committed** to God's message. He knew he had been called and gifted by God to proclaim the gospel of Christ. Faced with prison, Bunyan was offered a real-life 'get out of jail free' card; he could gain his freedom if he promised not to preach. He refused: he *had* to preach. It's easy to talk about 'opposition' to the Christian gospel today, but Bunyan knew real opposition and he stood firm. It's a great encouragement that the attempt to silence Bunyan by imprisoning him backfired in allowing him the opportunity to write. Bunyan's commitment to share the good news of Jesus whatever it costs is much needed today.

- Second, Bunyan **communicated** the message effectively and powerfully through *The Pilgrim's Progress*. Bunyan wrote in the language of everyday men and women and about ordinary people: his characters are individuals who we can all identify with. Bunyan wanted people to see themselves in his story and we do. Bunyan's book is a masterpiece on how to communicate the gospel and his skills are still needed.

Elstow in the
19th century.

- Third, Bunyan was **comprehensive** in his message. One reason for the lasting success of *The Pilgrim's Progress* is that it is not simply about how people should come to Christ but a guide to how they should live afterwards. Here conversion is not depicted as the end of the story but as the first step on what may be a long and challenging road. In *The Pilgrim's Progress* Bunyan writes something that has not just depth but breadth; he shows us the Christian life with all its delights and temptations, joys and challenges, struggles and victories. Bunyan was an evangelist to those outside the Christian faith and an encourager to those within it. There is a godly wisdom for us all in this.

- Finally, Bunyan was **caring** in his message. Bunyan was a pastor and had that essential gift for caring for people. He told the truth in love and for all the solemn warnings in *The Pilgrim's Progress* it is filled with empathy and concern. In particular there is comfort and encouragement to those who are finding the journey of faith a struggle. Jesus was described as the one who 'will not crush the weakest reed or put out a flickering candle' (Matthew 12:20 NLT). Bunyan imitated him and we should too.

Bunyan was a man who had indeed the ability 'to grip men's hearts'. He shared God's wisdom with an impact that few have equalled. If ever an age needed men and women like him, then it is ours.

GEORGE MÜLLER

One of the fascinating things about Christianity is how very different the great men and women of God are. George Müller (1805-1898) was not just different, he was unique.

Müller was born in the then Kingdom of Prussia (now Germany). He grew up into a young man who was frequently involved in petty crime, often to do with what we would call 'scams', and even a time in jail did nothing to reform him. However, in 1825 Müller attended a prayer meeting in someone's home where he encountered Christ. With his life dramatically transformed, Müller felt called to mission work and ended up in London working amongst Jews.

An illness led to him going to Devon to recover his health and that began life and ministry in the West Country. It became evident that he was gifted as a preacher and an evangelist, and he became the minister of a chapel. Soon he and his

Children playing in the Victorian period.

wife moved to Bristol. There he became involved in creating Christian schools and supporting missionaries. Müller established 117 schools which offered Christian education to tens of thousands of children, and he continued to support a great number of missionaries throughout his life.

Müller's Legacy

Müller is, however, remembered above all for his extraordinary achievements with orphans. In the Britain of the early nineteenth century the combination of large families, extreme poverty and a high level of adult mortality had resulted in many orphans, most of whom ended up on the street. The state ignored them and in 1836 Müller and his wife began taking them in. Their work grew in an astonishing way and they built a home for 300 children. Soon, however, even that was not enough, and more buildings followed in Bristol so that by 1870, 1,700 children were housed in five purpose-built homes with a total of 500 rooms.

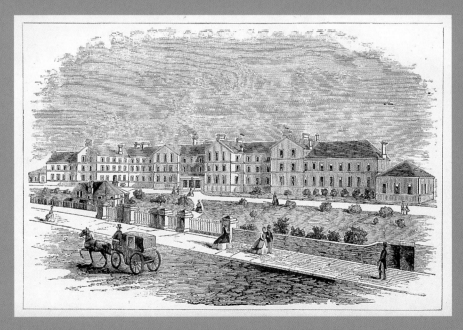

The third of five 'Müller Homes' built in the district of Ashley Down, in the north of Bristol. The five houses held 1,700 children at any one time.

Opened in 1864, Clifton Suspension Bridge, designed by Brunel, is one of Bristol's most recognisable structures.

By the end of Müller's life, his homes had housed 10,000 orphaned children. His commitment was not simply to house children but to clothe, feed and educate them and, ultimately, where possible, to find them jobs.

The Power of Prayer

This achievement alone would justify Müller's hero status, but what is astonishing is that in doing what he did he never made requests for financial support. He simply prayed that God would supply all his needs and left it to him to supply them. Extraordinarily, God did just that regularly and for decades. Müller was a meticulous administrator and his detailed accounts reveal that in his lifetime he received £1.5 million pounds in money and gifts; a figure that today would be over £100 million. Always astonishingly generous, he refused donations for his own well-being and died in near poverty.

These figures disguise an astonishing reality. There are many well-attested accounts of how, when he and his staff seemed to be on the point of running out of either food or money, last-minute unsolicited donations or gifts arrived. On one occasion Müller found himself with 300 orphans assembled for breakfast and no food at all. He simply sat them down at the table and confidently said grace. At this point, a knock at the door occurred. It was a local baker who had woken up at two o'clock in the morning with a feeling that he needed to bake more bread than usual and take it to the orphanage.

Shortly afterwards a milkman arrived to say that his wagon had broken down outside the orphanage and he wanted to offer his milk to the children. Over the decades, Müller's ever-expanding work often ran on a hand-to-mouth basis, but it never ran into debt.

His Final Years

With time Müller prayed for someone to succeed him as a manager and, having found him, handed over the reins in 1875. He then began seventeen years of missionary work across the world in which he travelled over 200,000 miles teaching and preaching. Müller's funeral in 1898 brought Bristol to a standstill with tens of thousands of people standing along the route. In a different form, his work continues today with the George Müller Charitable Trust.

Müller is a challenging figure in a number of areas but the most spectacular one is how he found funding for his work without openly asking for it. It's a strategy that many Christians have grappled with.

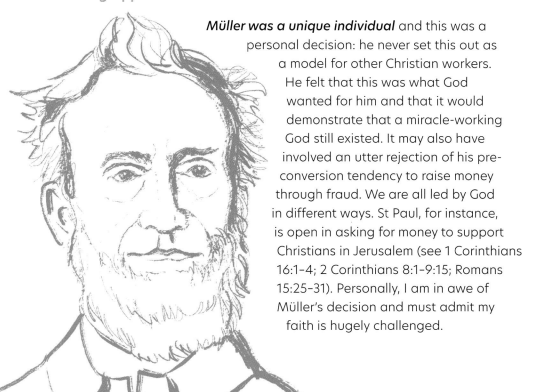

Müller was a unique individual and this was a personal decision: he never set this out as a model for other Christian workers. He felt that this was what God wanted for him and that it would demonstrate that a miracle-working God still existed. It may also have involved an utter rejection of his pre-conversion tendency to raise money through fraud. We are all led by God in different ways. St Paul, for instance, is open in asking for money to support Christians in Jerusalem (see 1 Corinthians 16:1-4; 2 Corinthians 8:1-9:15; Romans 15:25-31). Personally, I am in awe of Müller's decision and must admit my faith is hugely challenged.

I am reminded of my favourite George Müller quote:

'Faith does not operate in the realm of the possible. There is no glory for God in that which is humanly possible. Faith begins where man's power ends.'

Indeed that was true then and continues to be true today.

Yet there are other areas of Müller's life that are challenging.

- *His prayer life was astonishing*, and he had an extraordinarily deep relationship with God. Fundamental to this was how, despite running an enormous and complex charitable enterprise, he made sure that time with God came first.

- It's hard to not be impressed by the way that Müller's faith gave him breath-taking *audacity in what he planned and achieved*. Most of us would have been daunted by a goal of housing a hundred orphans, let alone a hundred times that.

- Finally, *Müller was committed to both preaching the gospel and doing good deeds*. He clearly felt no tension between sharing the good news of Jesus and working to care for orphans.

George Müller's unique life demonstrated to his contemporaries that God could be trusted. It says the same to us today.

Children at an orphanage in the Victorian era.

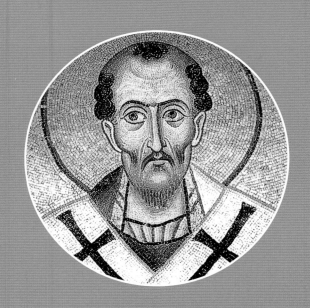

JOHN CHRYSOSTOM

When in the fourth century AD Christianity became the official religion of the Roman Empire, it lost the threat of persecution but gained new perils. As the church became popular, powerful and prosperous, a deadly formalism and corruption crept in. Into that troubled situation was born a man called John Chrysostom.

John was born in Antioch in Syria to a Greek family in AD 347. John was given a good education and learned rhetoric – the skill to speak effectively in public. After a reckless youth he turned to Christ in his twenties. He became a monk and lived such an austere lifestyle for several years that it affected his health. Of greater long-term benefit were his efforts to memorise the entire Bible. John moved from the monastic life for the church and became a priest in 386. For twelve years he remained in Antioch, preaching frequently and drawing large crowds. John was more than just a clever speaker. He spoke clearly to ordinary people with messages that were simple and practical and used illustrations from everyday life. He constantly appealed to the Bible as God-given authority. It is claimed that his eyes shone 'like burning torches'.

Antioch, the birthplace of John Chrysostom.

Modern-day Istanbul, formally Constantinople.

John was a gifted communicator and his sermons are some of the very few from the ancient world that can still be profitably read today. He also wrote many commentaries, showing the same common sense and practical application.

Constantinople

John had intended to stay in Antioch but the emperor felt that Constantinople, the eastern capital of the Roman Empire, needed someone of quality to occupy the pulpit. The result was that John was kidnapped in 398, taken to Constantinople and persuaded to be bishop. It was not a happy appointment! The authorities wanted a superstar preacher; instead they got a man of God.

Standing on the authority of the Bible, John sought to reform both the church and his society. Rejecting all attempts to pressure or limit him, he attacked extravagance and immorality and did all he could to deal with corruption within the church.

Left: Constantinople.

'Preaching improves me. When I begin to speak, weariness disappears; when I begin to teach, fatigue too disappears . . .'

JOHN CHRYSOSTOM

He preached against excessive wealth: 'It is foolishness and a public madness to fill the cupboards with clothing and allow men who are created in God's image and likeness to stand naked and trembling with the cold so that they can hardly hold themselves upright.' He practised what he preached. He sold off some of the art in the bishop's palace, refused to give lavish dinner parties, and criticised anything that involved excessive wealth and spending. Straightening out a corrupt financial system, John saved enough on his expenses in his first year to build a hospital for the poor.

A Divisive Figure

His attacks, not just against excessive wealth but against a whole range of social ills, gained him the friendship of the downtrodden and the hostility of the powerful. He refused to play politics and so it is hardly surprising that after five years he found himself banished from Constantinople to the edge of the Black Sea. There, in exile, he died in 407 and his last words were, 'Glory be to God in all things. Amen.'

Sixteen centuries lie between us and John Chrysostom and yet he still challenges us.

- First, *John was a model evangelist*. He had fire in his belly and logic in his brain; he preached Christ with urgency and life in a language that all could understand. He lived to proclaim the gospel and once said to his congregation,

'Preaching improves me. When I begin to speak, weariness disappears; when I begin to teach, fatigue too disappears . . .' There was, too, an extraordinary urgency to his message. As he said, 'There is nothing colder than a Christian who does not seek to save others.'

- Second, **John was also an evangelist with vision**. In marked contrast to most of his contemporaries he saw beyond his own city and community, sending out church planters into the Danube Valley and eastwards to what is now Iran.

- Third, **John was a man who preached that right beliefs had to be matched with right actions**. He wanted to see his society and his church cleaned up.

- Fourth, **John was a biblical man**. He took his stand on Scripture and taught that it had supreme authority. He encouraged his hearers to read the Bible too.

- Finally, **John proclaimed a simple lifestyle**. He consistently opposed excess wealth and self-indulgent luxury.

John Chrysostom is an awesome figure. In troubled times he spoke out for an authentic Christianity: a faith centred on Christ, guided by the Bible and utterly independent of every pressure of culture. John was indeed a 'golden mouth' for the gospel. Our age needs more men and women like him today.

The Church of Saint Peter in Antioch is one of the oldest churches in the world with some sections dating to the 4th or 5th century BC.

MARY JONES

Mary Jones was born in December 1784 at Llanfihangel-y-Pennant, a small hamlet in one of the deep valleys of North Wales. It was a Welsh-speaking, sheep-farming community and Mary's family earned a meagre living from the weaving of wool. Life got harder after Mary's father died when she was four.

Wales had been affected by several revivals in the eighteenth century and Mary grew up in a Christian home. One man who was involved in preaching at the revivals was Reverend Thomas Charles. He was not just a powerful preacher but also someone responsible for creating a basic school system in the area.

In 1791 he found himself at the heart of another wave of revival. He wrote, 'Here, in our town of Bala, for some time back, we have had a very great, powerful, and glorious outpouring of the Spirit of God, on the people in general, especially young people. The state and welfare of the soul is become the general concern of the country. Scores of the wildest, and most inconsiderate of the people, have been awakened.' One Sunday he wrote, 'About nine o'clock at night, there was nothing to be heard from one end of the town to the other, but the cries and groans of people in distress of soul.'

Reverend Thomas Charles.

The revival spread quickly and widely around the surrounding area bringing with it not just conversions but also a deepening and enriching of people's Christian faith. It is in this atmosphere that, a year after the revival, Mary came to profess the Christian faith at the age of eight. Courtesy of one of Thomas Charles' schools, Mary was able to read and soon wanted a Bible for herself. Welsh Bibles were rare and expensive and the nearest copy available was owned by a neighbour two miles away. Mary would regularly walk over to read and memorise all she could, but she soon began saving for a Bible of her own.

Inspiring a Movement

Six years later she had enough money. Hearing that Bibles could be obtained from Thomas Charles in Bala, twenty-six miles away on rugged roads, she set out barefoot one morning in 1800 to buy one. Mary returned home the delighted possessor of a Bible.

What then happened was that Thomas Charles, pondering on her hunger and action to get the Word of God, proposed the formation of a society to supply Wales with reasonably priced Bibles. His proposal expanded: why just Wales? Why not other parts of the United Kingdom? Indeed, why not the world? And in 1804 the British and Foreign Bible Society (now the Bible Society) was formed. There's a story that, at the age of seventy, Mary Jones gave half a sovereign – a significant amount in those days – towards the Bible Society's appeal to print a million Chinese New Testaments.

Exact copy of Mary Jones' Bible.

In the story of Mary Jones, I see three things that both encourage and challenge me.

• First, *Mary Jones' confidence in the Bible and her hunger to possess it*. Clearly, she prized it as something that was so valuable that it was worth years of saving and hours of walking because she knew the Bible revealed Jesus. Do we treat God's Word with this respect? We ought to.

The road to Lake Bala.

• Second, ***Mary Jones demonstrates one of the great themes of the Bible***: that the mighty God works through little people. It would be hard to find anybody more insignificant at the end of the eighteenth century than this poor girl in a remote corner of Wales. Yet God took her zeal and commitment and used it to set in progress something that was to have an extraordinary effect on the world and continues to have today through 140 Bible Societies all over the world. Let us seize the opportunities that 'little people' give us.

• Finally, ***we see the working of the Holy Spirit in revival***. God's Spirit was at work in preparing a people who hungered for God and his Word. God spoke in extraordinary power, convicting people of their sin and pointing them to Jesus. Our world needs that sort of spiritual revival today. Let's pray for it!

AUGUSTINE OF HIPPO

St Augustine may be 'the most influential figure in Christianity after St Paul'. He wrote much (some 5 million words), and his teaching has influenced theology ever since.

Like all of us, Augustine was of his time and place. He lived through the proverbial 'interesting times'. He was born in AD 354, three decades after the ending of the persecution of Christians by a pagan Roman Empire, and died seventy-five years later with the now Christian empire tumbling around him. He was born in North Africa, spent most of his life in Algeria and considered himself an African.

A Journey of Faith

We know quite a bit about the young Augustine because of his famous *Confessions*. He grew up under a devoted Christian mother and, clearly gifted, progressed through a succession of teaching positions, spending time in Rome and Milan. Yet Augustine was disturbed by the need to find meaning in life and in search of it he pursued various religions and philosophies.

Eventually, drawn by a sense of emptiness, Augustine, now in his early thirties, turned back towards Christianity. The *Confessions* tell how, in the middle of his agonised indecision, he heard children's voices telling him to 'take up and read'. So prompted, he opened his

*'Lord, you have made us for yourself,
and our heart is restless until it rests in you.'*

AUGUSTINE OF HIPPO

Bible at Romans 13:13-14: 'Let us behave decently, as in the daytime, not in carousing and drunkenness, not in sexual immorality and debauchery, not in dissension and jealousy. Rather, clothe yourselves with the Lord Jesus Christ, and do not think about how to gratify the desires of the flesh.'

Augustine made his choice and, with characteristic determination, devoted himself to the Christian life. He renounced his marriage plans, was baptised and returned to North Africa in AD 388 to create a lay monastic community. There, somewhat against his will, he was ordained and soon became Bishop of Hippo, now Annaba in Algeria. It was a position he held for forty years until he died.

St Augustine in His Study (Vittore Carpaccio, 1502)

Influencing History

As bishop, Augustine faced many difficulties. There were bitter debates over whether to accept back into fellowship those who, under persecution, had denied the faith. There were theological challenges over the extent to which men and women could make themselves right with God. Augustine dealt with them all as well as applying himself to reforming his churches and training future leaders. He set a personal example for commitment, writing, 'A bishop who has set his heart on a position of eminence rather than an opportunity for service should realise that he is no bishop.'

A mosaic of Saint Augustine of Hippo, located in the Church of the Beatitudes by the Sea of Galilee in Israel.

Somehow, though, Augustine – preacher, pastor and administrator – managed to be a prolific writer of books including evil, time, history, warfare and the Trinity.

In his latter years, Augustine faced a world in turmoil. With Christianity now the state religion, most believers saw the Empire as central to God's purposes on earth and Rome as the 'eternal city'. Inevitably then, when Rome fell to the Goths in AD 410, the impact on the faithful was catastrophic, made worse by pagan accusations that the Christian God had failed. Augustine's response was a massive book, *The City of God*, in which he pointed out that Christian hope lay not in any earthly state or city but only in heaven, the eternal city of God.

As the Empire crumbled further, Vandal tribes arrived in North Africa. Augustine died literally with the barbarians at the gate as they besieged Hippo in AD 430. His library, however, survived and was copied to become the foundation of subsequent Christian thinking.

The St Augustin Basilica, located in Annaba, Algeria, and dedicated to St Augustine of Hippo.

So what do I admire in Augustine?

- Obviously *I'm impressed by his all-round intellect*, but even more that it didn't stop him from his church ministry. Augustine was that rarity: a genius who was prepared to be a servant.

Yet there is more.

- *I am encouraged by how Augustine came to faith*. We see someone who, faced with the challenge of Christ, chose to respond and produced a changed life as a result. We evangelists are often accused of talking up the 'conversion experience'. I appeal to Augustine in our defence.

- *I am challenged by Augustine's deep analysis of the human condition*. He wrote a lot about sin and how it has corrupted every aspect of our being. His bleak warning of the flawed nature of every one of us should never be neglected. We all need to be saved! But Augustine didn't stop at guilt; he saw beyond it to the ultimate emptiness of the godless life. I have quoted many times his prayer from the *Confessions*:

> *'Lord, you have made us for yourself,*
> *and our heart is restless until it rests in you.'*

There, in a single brilliant phrase, is the human dilemma. Thankfully, too, Augustine did not just proclaim sin but he proclaimed its remedy: salvation through grace. Augustine taught salvation is God's gift in Christ.

- Finally, living in a turbulent age, I find myself uplifted by *how Augustine responded to the turmoil of his time*. If ever there was a case of 'the end of the world as we know it' it was the fall of Rome. Yet sustained by Scripture, Augustine stood firm and pointed beyond the upheaval of the world to the eternal City of God. That's a vision we urgently need to recapture and proclaim!

Coat of arms of the Order of Saint Augustine, 1910.

ROBERT MURRAY M'CHEYNE

The saying 'it's not the years of your life that matter, it's the life in your years' was never move true of anyone than Robert Murray M'Cheyne who died at only twenty-nine.

M'Cheyne, who was born in Edinburgh in 1813, had a formal Christian faith. Well educated, M'Cheyne became a student of classics at the University of Edinburgh. There, for the first few years, he pursued an active social life and was, by his own later admission, careless about God and spiritual matters.

Everything changed in 1831 when David, his eldest brother, died aged just twenty-seven. David had been depressed but just before his death had found peace through Christ and had begun to pray for his brother. A new seriousness gripped M'Cheyne; he began to question his spiritual state and started going to a church where the gospel was preached. Soon he accepted Christ as Saviour and applied to be a minister in the Church of Scotland. He began his theological training at Edinburgh.

Edinburgh today.

Finishing his training, M'Cheyne served as an assistant in a church near Falkirk. In 1836, after less than a year, he moved to Dundee as a minister of St Peter's Church. It was a demanding situation in a poor, heavily populated and industrial area. M'Cheyne's poor health – he may already have had tuberculosis – was not helped by the location.

A Life Well Lived

It soon became apparent to his church that this was no ordinary minister. For all his youth, M'Cheyne was a powerful preacher; his sermons were biblical, compassionate and compelling. M'Cheyne spoke clearly and simply. Yet it was the person as much as the preacher that seems to have had an impact; M'Cheyne was someone who knew God personally and it was obvious to people. He worked hard as a pastor, regularly visiting homes to talk about Jesus and, where necessary, writing people discerning letters. Poor health regularly forced M'Cheyne to take time off which he used for praying, Scripture reading and letter writing. Such times heightened his feeling that he had only a few years to live and gave his ministry an urgency.

St Peter's Church, Dundee.

It's easy to imagine M'Cheyne as a solitary man. The reality is, however, that he was deeply loved by his congregation and his many friends, who included fellow ministers. He never married, but he did have a fiancée at the time of his death.

In 1839 M'Cheyne was sent, along with three other ministers, to Palestine for an eight-month ministry trip. During M'Cheyne's absence, an 'awakening' – a revival – occurred in his church.

Much of M'Cheyne's ministry took place in the Scottish city of Dundee.

There were many conversions and the deep rededication of those who were already Christians. This atmosphere of revival continued into the all too brief remaining years of M'Cheyne's ministry at St Peter's. In 1843, at the age of twenty-nine and just seven years of ministry, M'Cheyne caught typhus and died. His impact was such that at his funeral 6,000 people lined the streets.

His Legacy

Death did not end M'Cheyne's influence. Within two years Andrew Bonar, a close friend and fellow minister, produced a book entitled *The Memoir and Remains of the Rev. Robert Murray M'Cheyne*. (The 'Remains' were some of M'Cheyne's letters and sermons.) It is a spiritual classic that has helped many people and never been out of print. It deeply impacted me when I was at theological college.

Left: Edinburgh in the 19th century.

To read about M'Cheyne is to be humbled. What was the secret to his extraordinary ministry? A foundation was his knowledge and love of the Bible. Here M'Cheyne gave the world an important bequest in designing a system for reading through the Bible in one year. My wife Killy and I follow it. I do recommend that you try it.

There was more, though, than just a profound biblical knowledge behind M'Cheyne's remarkable ministry. Let me suggest four things that were important and which challenge and inspire me.

- First, *M'Cheyne was a man of purity*. Holiness may not be talked about today but it was essential for M'Cheyne. He wrote, 'The greatest need of my people is my personal holiness' and 'Lord, make me as holy as a pardoned sinner can be.' He advised those who preach the gospel to 'study universal holiness of life. Your whole usefulness depends on this, for your sermons last but an hour or two; your life preaches all the week.' M'Cheyne didn't simply seek the experience of knowing Christ; he sought to be like him.

Andrew Bonar who produced the spiritual classic *The Memoir and Remains of the Rev. Robert Murray M'Cheyne.*

- Second, *M'Cheyne was a man of prayer*. M'Cheyne had an extended period of prayer before he did anything else in the day. For him prayer was not a duty but a pleasure; he basked in the love of Christ. He also felt that he was being prayed for:

'If I could hear Christ praying for me in the next room, I would not fear a million enemies. Yet distance makes no difference. He is praying for me.'

- Third, **M'Cheyne was a man of perception**. M'Cheyne had a deep insight into both God and people. He was perceptive in his preaching; discerning what his congregation needed to hear and teaching it. For instance, fully aware of the tendency to look too deeply into oneself, he wrote, 'For every look at self, take ten looks at Christ.' Above all, though, he was perceptive of heavenly realities, in particular the imminence of death and what comes after: 'Live for eternity. A few days more and our journey is done.'

- Finally, **M'Cheyne was a man of passion**. Throughout all he did ran an extraordinary commitment and urgency: 'I have never risen a morning without thinking how I could bring more souls to Christ.' His passion drove him and also helped convince his hearers. In one sense typhus killed M'Cheyne; in another he simply let himself burn out for Christ.

Robert Murray M'Cheyne was a remarkable man. Ultimately, he didn't just preach Christ, he demonstrated Christ. As he himself said, 'It is not great talents God blesses so much as great likeness to Jesus.' And if that doesn't challenge and inspire you, I don't know what will.

WILLIAM SEYMOUR

William Seymour was at the heart of the Azusa Street Revival that reshaped Christianity across the world. If you are one of the half a billion Christians who are now a Pentecostal or a Charismatic then your roots lie in that revival, and even if you are not, how you worship and sing in church will have been influenced by it.

William Seymour was born in 1870 in Louisiana to former slaves who lived in extreme poverty. After a very limited education, he came to Christ in an African-American church. He caught smallpox, which blinded him in one eye, and afterwards dedicated himself to God as a preacher. Seymour became part of a movement that believed in being 'baptised in the Spirit', something seen by many then (and now) as a life-transforming, post-conversion experience for a Christian. (My own view is that every Christian needs to grow in their faith, whether by an event, events or a process.)

A slave's house in New Orleans, Louisiana. The type of house William Seymour may have lived in as a child.

Seymour was invited to pastor a mission in Los Angeles. He started an African-American prayer group in a home. After extensive times of prayer, several of the participants, including Seymour, began speaking in tongues. His group grew rapidly and in 1906 took over a derelict church building at 312 Azusa Street, in what was then a rundown part of Los Angeles.

Revival on Azusa Street

This was a time when there was an expectancy of revival. The Welsh Revival of 1904–1905, with 100,000 conversions and remarkable phenomena, had been reported worldwide and there had been revivals in India and Madagascar. As Seymour pastored his fellowship, revival broke out. At what soon became nearly continuous meetings there was spontaneous worship, fervent prayer, public repentance, conversions and healings. Above all, there was a sacred sense of the powerful presence of God. Soon, news of what was happening spread both by word-of-mouth and through the press – who were not just critical of the 'one-eyed black minister' and the 'fanaticism' but also offended by what were soon remarkably interracial meetings. Crowds of 1,500 regularly attended Azusa Street.

Aerial view of the downtown area of Azusa, California, today.

18

Originally drawing from the poor, dispossessed and the African-American community, the meetings soon attracted people from every race and social level. Visitors came first from the United States and then from around the world, returning home renewed and with the expectancy for similar revivals.

Whilst this went on, Seymour remained pastor and preacher; in the gentlest way encouraging unity and equality. He never over-emphasised the phenomena that occurred, saying,

'Don't go out of here talking about tongues; talk about Jesus.'

Apostolic Faith Movement

He had the wisdom (and humility) to surround himself with a capable, interracial staff of men and women who were able to expand the impact of Azusa Street. With them, Seymour started the Apostolic Faith Movement and produced an influential newsletter that became widely circulated nationally and globally.

Seymour believed that what was happening was a second Pentecost and a potential precursor to Christ's Second Coming. As the first Pentecost had led to the gospel going out to the world so, he believed, should this. Evangelists with the power of God experiences at Azusa Street were sent out across the States. Soon 'Pentecostal' missionaries went out across the world and within two years the movement had spread to over fifty nations.

Let me tell you why William Seymour is a hero of the faith.

• First, **Seymour had a spiritual hunger.** He had a 'holy dissatisfaction' with the state of Christianity personally, nationally and globally. He wanted

Leaders of the Apostolic Faith Mission.

his own life, and that of the church worldwide, to better reflect the pattern that he saw in the book of Acts: overflowing with purity and power from the Holy Spirit. Today,we all need that hunger to know more of the presence, purity and power of God.

• Second, **Seymour had humility**. Every description speaks of him as being a soft-spoken, unassuming, gentle and friendly man, prepared even to allow his critics to speak to his congregation. Although the leader of the Azusa Street Revival he never sought 'star status'. Revivals are God's work and while I believe that human beings cannot cause revivals, I'm fairly certain that they can block them. Quite simply, Seymour didn't get in God's way.

• Finally, **Seymour sought harmony**. He avoided antagonism but, specifically, taught that any church on which God was pouring out his Spirit should avoid discriminating on race or gender. He strongly believed racial unity in worship was important; indeed, he felt it was a sure sign of God's blessing. In these days that's an emphasis that would be good to recover.

William Seymour was an astonishingly important man. It's a measure of him that being forgotten is something that wouldn't have bothered him. His main desire was to know Christ and make him known. I can't think of a better one.

CORRIE TEN BOOM

When I became a Christian in 1975 one book that everybody read was Corrie ten Boom's The Hiding Place. *I read it in one sitting – I couldn't put it down. Although less read today, it remains an outstanding testimony to courage, faith and forgiveness.*

Corrie ten Boom was born in Amsterdam in 1892 into one of those wonderful, godly families where faith goes back generations. Her upbringing – lovingly described in her books – included a saintly father who was a skilled watchmaker, and a sister, Betsie, of deep spiritual insight. The family atmosphere was one filled with prayer and care that extended out into the community. Corrie's family were well known for generosity and had a particularly good relationship with the Jews around them who they considered 'God's ancient people'.

Corrie followed her father, becoming in 1922 the first female watchmaker in the Netherlands. In the 1920s and 1930s she and her family applied their Christian faith through Bible studies and youth clubs, including some for children with disabilities.

Haarlem in the Netherlands, where Corrie ten Boom was born.

Posters of the Dutch resistance during the Second World War.

When the Netherlands was brutally invaded by the Nazis in 1940, those deep links with the community meant that Corrie and her family became involved in protecting those whom the invaders wanted to seize. They took in Jews and members of the Dutch resistance and, after hiding them within the house, passed them on to the underground network.

The Hiding Place

Within months, Corrie found herself associated with the resistance and involved in risky schemes to obtain enough food in a time of rationing. A secret chamber – the physical 'hiding place' of the book – that could take six people was installed behind a false wall in Corrie's bedroom.

A recruitment poster for the Dutch SS, an extension of the paramilitary organisation under Nazi Germany.

As the Nazi occupation tightened, the role – and the risk – of Corrie's home being a 'safe house' increased. The family was betrayed and in February 1944 all of them, along with thirty other people, were arrested and taken to prison.

Ordeal

For Corrie, aged fifty-two, the real ordeal began. She was held in solitary confinement, learning after several weeks that her father had died but that the Jews in the 'hiding place' were safe. Reunited with Betsie, she was then sent to a political camp and finally on to the Ravensbrück concentration camp in Germany, where women prisoners were either used as forced labour or executed. Here the health of Betsie, who had always been weak, deteriorated and she died on 16th December 1944 at the age of fifty-nine.

Entrance to the hiding place where Jews were hidden during World War Two.

Fifteen days later, Corrie was released, seemingly as a result of a 'clerical error'. A week afterwards, all the women in her age group were sent to the gas chambers. After a painful journey back to the Netherlands, she was reunited with the surviving members of her family and, with the war coming to an end, opened her home to those in need, this time many with mental disabilities.

After the war Corrie set up a rehabilitation centre, caring for both victims of concentration camps but also those despised individuals who had collaborated with the Germans. She soon began an itinerant evangelistic ministry which grew rapidly. One challenge that she faced was encountering a German guard who had been cruel to Betsie at Ravensbrück and finding that she could forgive him.

CORRIE TEN BOOM

For nearly thirty years Corrie preached worldwide, visiting more than sixty countries. In 1971 her book *The Hiding Place* was published and became a best-seller. In 1977 Corrie moved to California where, after a long illness, she died in 1983 at the age of ninety-one.

It has been estimated that with her family and neighbours, Corrie ten Boom saved the lives of 800 Jews and other refugees. She was honoured by Israel for her work as one of the 'Righteous Among the Nations'.

The life and witness of Corrie ten Boom gives us a lot to think about, not least her courage and her ability to forgive. I think what strikes me is the all-round richness of her faith. Let me note four things.

• First, *Corrie's faith had a foundation*. Some people looking at Corrie ten Boom might see what she did as a result of her 'faith'. In fact, as almost every page of *The Hiding Place* reveals, her faith was built on Jesus Christ. What she did was based on how Jesus had lived, how he had suffered and how he had risen triumphant over death and evil. When one woman told Corrie that 'her faith' must have brought her through, Corrie simply replied, 'No, it was Jesus!'

Corrie ten Boom with actress Jeannette Clift who played the part of Corrie in the 1975 film *The Hiding Place*.

● Second, **Corrie's faith had a solid formation**. Corrie had been a Christian for well over forty years before the storm of the Second World War broke over her. It must have seemed unlikely to this quiet, unmarried repairer of watches that she would ever need heroism or to endure brutality. Yet, as her books reveal, in those decades she had built up deep spiritual resources from constant prayer, Bible reading and worship. It's a wise principle to build a strong faith: none of us knows what we will have to face in the future.

The house where Corrie ten Boom lived and hid Jews during World War Two. Now the Corrie ten Boom Museum.

● Third, **Corrie's faith gave rise to intervention**. Corrie had a deep, rich faith but she is remembered by history because she lived out what she believed. She was involved in numerous activities to serve others before the war; the crisis of the occupation simply added risk and urgency to what she was already doing. Corrie's life, faith and actions were seamlessly linked.

● Finally, **Corrie's faith gave her perception**. Corrie learnt to look at situations from God's perspective. So, she was able to be compassionate to those who abused her because she could see how God saw them. She stayed active in preaching when she could have retired because she realised that people needed to know Jesus. Her personal faith gave her a perspective that made her stand apart from others.

Corrie ten Boom was someone who stood firm and served Jesus Christ – her true 'hiding place' – faithfully in her time. May we do the same in ours.

Corrie ten Boom was the first female watchmaker in the Netherlands.

57

CHARLES SIMEON

Many Christian heroes made a difference to the world by travelling it; Charles Simeon made a difference by staying in the same place ministering for fifty-four years.

Simeon was born in 1759 to a wealthy, upper-class family in the south-east of England who had only a superficial Christian faith. Educated at Eton and King's College, Cambridge, as a young man Simeon was wealthy, witty, vain and short-tempered, with few interests outside riding, sport and fashion.

At Cambridge, he discovered the uncomfortable fact that the university required him to take Holy Communion at Easter. Contemplating this, Simeon found himself overwhelmed with his own unworthiness and feeling that 'Satan himself was as fit to attend as I'. Without anyone to guide him, he turned to the Bible and Christian books to find out how he could make himself right with God. Finally, he came to the joyful realisation that, at the cross, Christ had done for him what he could not do for himself. In the spiritual darkness of the period, Simeon grew in his faith and felt called to be a preacher of the gospel and his thoughts turned to a local church, Holy Trinity Church in the centre of Cambridge.

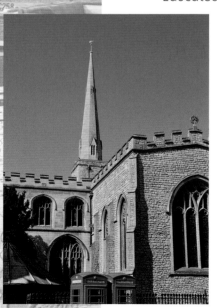

Holy Trinity Church, Cambridge.

(Here can I admit a personal interest? It's where I met my wife Killy – the then-vicar's daughter – when I led a mission in Cambridge in 1981! My father-in-law Reverend Canon Michael Rees was the vicar of Holy Trinity 1972–1984, and Killy and I got married at Holy Trinity on 23rd July 1983.)

Holy Trinity, Cambridge

In fact, through some unusual circumstances, Simeon, still not fully ordained, found himself given responsibility for Holy Trinity at the age of twenty-two. His irregular appointment, his youth, his somewhat curious mannerisms and his earnest preaching made him unpopular with the congregation who, at first, opposed him in every manner possible. Confident that this was where God wanted him, Simeon resisted opposition and ended up being the vicar of Holy Trinity for fifty-four years until his death.

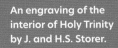

An engraving of the interior of Holy Trinity by J. and H.S. Storer.

Simeon worked hard at his preaching and pastoring and increasingly his ministry came to be appreciated. His congregation steadily grew until eventually he was preaching twice on Sunday with over a thousand people attending. Ever practical, he created a support team with twenty-four pastoral assistants, both men and women. As he continued in his church, he remained as a resident of King's College in rooms that offered him a useful venue for meeting with students and those interested in the Christian faith. From his fixed position in Cambridge, Simeon began to exert an ever-increasing influence for the gospel.

King's College, Cambridge.

He took a particular interest in encouraging young men with potential for the ministry, teaching them theology and preaching skills. With time, his protégés became clerics in the Church of England and, as they did, his own reputation spread.

Simeon was always eager to support Christian ventures and was a founder of both the Church Church Missionary Society and, with William Wilberforce, what is now the Church's Ministry Among Jewish People or CMJ.

An Incredible Legacy

He was a great supporter of missionaries, many of whom, including the remarkable Henry Martyn, he knew well personally.

Simeon died in 1836, just a few months before the start of Queen Victoria's reign. Much had changed during his long ministry. Within Cambridge he was now an honoured and respected figure; indeed, the town came to a stop for his funeral. Within the British nation, the evangelical beliefs that he had promoted were now mainstream. At the time of Simeon's death, it is estimated that one-third of all the Anglican ministers in the country had sat under his teaching at one time or another and Simeon's biblical Christianity was to become a profound influence on the moral tone of the Victorian period. And worldwide, there were Christians who had either been converted by Simeon or whom he had taught and trained.

Charles Simeon was a man of priorities and three strike me powerfully.

- First, ***Simeon made prayer a priority.*** His pattern was to get up at four o'clock in the morning and spend four hours in prayer and Bible reading.

The enormous amount that Simeon achieved was built on the firmest of foundations: a rich and deep personal relationship with God.

- Second, ***Simeon made preaching a priority***. He saw faithful, clear, biblical preaching as one of the main ways in which the kingdom of God advanced. He worked hard at his preaching, taking hours in sermon preparation and always being careful to make sure that what he said was rooted in Scripture and focused on Christ.

He preached effectively and taught others to do the same. In order to help other preachers, he published his sermon outlines which ran to twenty-one volumes.

- ***Simeon made posterity a priority***. He took a strategic view of how to spread the gospel. He didn't simply want people to be just converted; he wanted them to be those who would go on to preach the gospel to others. He preached, taught and counselled individuals and used every means he could to find parishes for them.

Quietly, steadily, unspectacularly, Sunday by Sunday, Charles Simeon spent his life preaching. Through his preaching, God used him in an astonishing way to change both his nation and the world for good.

AMY CARMICHAEL

Amy Carmichael (1867–1951) was an evangelist and a social reformer who worked for a better life for women and girls and fought against the sexual trafficking and abuse of children.

Amy was born in County Down, Ireland in 1867 and grew up in a devout Christian family. At the age of fifteen she committed her life to Christ and soon, in a foreshadowing of her future, became involved in an evangelistic and social ministry to mill girls in Belfast. At twenty-one, Amy heard Hudson Taylor of the China Inland Mission speak and felt called to missionary work.

Initially her attempts to get on the mission field did not go smoothly. Barely five-foot tall and suffering from a number of ailments (some of which were to permanently plague her), she was rejected for work in China. Undeterred, she applied to another society and

Carmichael was born in Millisle, County Down.

then spent time in Japan, China and Sri Lanka before finally arriving in southern India in 1895. Once there, she put down roots and never left until she died fifty-five years later.

Amy started her work with poor, lower-caste girls and soon became aware of those who had been forced to become a *devadasi*, a 'religious prostitute', in local temples. In 1901, Amy met a seven-year-old girl who had escaped from the temple and needed to be protected. She realised that preaching against the evil of child abuse wasn't enough: she needed to provide a 'safe place' for those she rescued. The result was a settlement – the Dohnavur Fellowship – which by 1913 was already looking after 130 girls. After the First World War, Amy opened a home for young boys, many of whom had been born to temple prostitutes. Guided by her own happy experience of family life, Amy worked to ensure that her orphanages never became institutions but instead were 'family'. She herself became universally called '*Amma*' or 'mother' in Tamil.

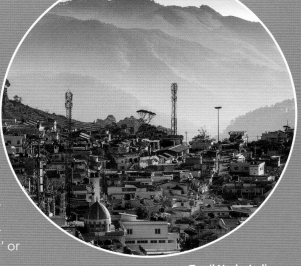

Tamil Nadu, India, where Carmichael founded the Dohnavur Fellowship.

Ahead of Her Time

Amy's work faced both opposition and apathy. Indeed she even found coolness towards her work from the mission societies who felt that the evils she battled against were not what their supporters wanted to hear about. Amy found herself independent of any mission organisation.

One of the many fascinating features about Amy is how, in many ways, she was decades ahead of her time. She saw the problems with institutional orphanages and tried instead to create a family atmosphere. She was profoundly sensitive to cultural issues and adapted to local culture as much as she could, dressing in local clothes and cosmetically darkening her skin. She was very wary of uncritically

importing western ideals and habits to replace traditional Indian practices and worked towards an authentic Indian Christianity. She was particularly careful that her criticism of the *devadasi* system could not be misunderstood as an attack on traditional Indian values.

Amy suffered a serious fall in 1931 and remained bedbound at Dohnavur for the remaining twenty years of her life. Typically, she refused to waste the time, involving herself in prayer and in writing thirty-five books. Her writings reveal a profound faith, deepened and refined by suffering. Amy has contributed many quotations to the Christian world and here are some of my favourites.

'Prayer is the core of the day. Take prayer out, and the day would collapse.'

'If you have never been hurt by a word from God, it is probably that you have never heard God speak.'

'The saddest thing one meets is a nominal Christian.'

Amy asked that no gravestone be erected to her, and all that exists over her grave is a birdbath inscribed with that single word *'Amma'*. Of course, her real monument is the Dohnavur Fellowship which continues to this day. Sadly, so does temple prostitution, despite being technically outlawed. And, of course, throughout the world, prostitution and trafficking of children continues, particularly where there is poverty.

'One can give without loving, but one cannot love without giving'

AMY CARMICHAEL

Amy was a remarkable woman who challenges me in a number of areas.

- First, *I'm challenged by Amy's focus*. Amy felt called to take care of orphans and, for fifty years, that's exactly what she did. To use one of her images, she chose to plough deep rather than wide. She let nothing distract her.

- Second, *I'm challenged by how forceful Amy was*. Amy faced extraordinary obstacles throughout her life. Her health was frail, her supporters often critical and her exposure of difficult and sensitive matters antagonised the British authorities who preferred to overlook what happened to poor, low-caste girls in India. Yet Amy, undeterred, continued her work. She let nothing divert her.

- Finally, *I'm challenged by Amy's frankness*. The first book Amy wrote from India in 1905 was titled *Things as They Are*. In it, she spoke with honesty about the state of affairs in southern India and was denounced for doing so. She could be forthright: when a woman wrote asking, 'What is missionary life like?' she received the reply, 'Missionary life is simply a chance to die.' At times, Amy accused some of her fellow Christians of merely 'playing at mission'. Amy spoke out and she let nothing dilute her.

Amy Carmichael was an extraordinary woman. To be honest, I'm not sure I would have found Amy a comfortable colleague. But she was clearly the individual God wanted to do that task in that time and place. That raises a question: are we where we ought to be and are we focused, forceful and frank?

EDWARD JENNER

It has been said of Edward Jenner that 'his work saved more lives than any other man on earth'. It's an extraordinary claim for someone who spent his entire life as a country doctor.

Edward Jenner was born in 1749 in Berkeley, Gloucestershire, England, the son of the local vicar. His family had a long tradition of sending people into the church, but the death of Jenner's father left the family impoverished and forced the young man to take up another career. From an early age Jenner had a great interest in science and the natural world and was apprenticed to a doctor. Learning the trade, he went on to work in London where his skills both as a physician and a scientist were soon recognised. He was invited by Captain Cook to be part of the science team on his second voyage to Australasia. Jenner, however, had no love of either travel or London life and soon returned to his home village as its doctor.

Jenner's reputation as a caring and wise doctor grew among his community but he continued to pursue his long-standing fascination with nature. He was particularly interested in birds and his careful studies of cuckoo behaviour gained him such respect in the British scientific community that he was elected to the prestigious Royal Society.

The Chantry, Edward Jenner's house in Berkeley.

The great medical curse of the age was the killer disease smallpox. In Europe, around 400,000 people a year died from the disease. Typically, when smallpox swept through a village 20 to 50 per cent of those infected died. A third of the survivors of smallpox went blind and many more were scarred for life.

People were so desperate to avoid smallpox that they sought to be deliberately inoculated from sores of those who had a mild form of the disease in the hope that this would give them some immunity. It was a risky procedure with limited success: the great American preacher Jonathan Edwards died as a result of it. It was a disease without a cure.

Vaccination

In thinking about smallpox, Jenner pondered a dairymaid's intriguing comment: 'I shall never have smallpox for I have had cowpox.' Cowpox was a mild infection in animals which could be caught by humans with little harmful effect. Jenner concluded that there must be a possibility that smallpox could be prevented by inoculating people with cowpox. Yet as a scientist he knew that to be of any worth, any experiments had to be conducted carefully. When an outbreak of cowpox occurred locally, Jenner deliberately inoculated a young stable-hand with it. The boy suffered only mild effects and when, a few months later, he was inoculated with smallpox, he failed to catch the far more serious disease.

Jenner's study of cuckoo behaviour gained him significant respect in the British scientific community.

Encouraged, Jenner persisted with more inoculations and in 1797 sent a short communication to the Royal Society describing his results. His paper was rejected on the grounds that it had only thirteen samples. Disappointed but not deterred, Jenner went away and carried out more work, eventually publishing his results at his own expense.

Jenner called his new procedure *vaccination* after the Latin word for cow, *vacca*. Despite controversy, his method spread rapidly throughout Britain and was soon taken up across the world. Jenner refused to make money out of his discovery – he vaccinated the poor for free – and in encouraging the careful use of the new technique he bankrupted himself.

There is very little to say about the rest of Jenner's life. He continued as a doctor and consultant, kept up his interest in the natural world and died in 1823. His old adversary, smallpox, outlasted him but not for long. Increasingly confined to remote parts of the world, it was finally eradicated in 1980.

Despite the turbulence of the times in which Jenner lived – the Napoleonic wars were raging – his fame became enormous. He was soon considered one of the most famous men in Europe and honoured everywhere, even by Napoleon, who had his entire army vaccinated.

Cartoon by James Gillray (1802) depicting vaccinations against smallpox.

Christian Faith

Edward Jenner was a committed Christian. He was typical of many believers in every age who demonstrate their faith through the way they live their lives. An amiable, quiet, warm-hearted Christian, ever ready with the appropriate Bible verse, Jenner was anxious that his discovery would be used as widely as possible. He was particularly concerned that praise should be directed not to him, but to the God who had made and used him.

A panoramic view of the Severn Valley, close to Berkeley where Jenner lived.

I find many challenges in the life of Edward Jenner.

- First, *I'm challenged by what Jenner achieved*. In Christian circles, it is still sometimes held that the highest calling anyone can have is that of being a full-time minister of the gospel. Circumstances demanded that Jenner never made it as a preacher but it's hard to imagine a life of greater value than his.

- Second, *I'm challenged by how Jenner let his Christianity guide his work as a doctor and a scientist*. His faith supported and regulated all that he did as a doctor and scientist. His science – apparently still impressive two centuries on – overflowed with virtues: enquiring, accurate and honest.

- Third, *I'm challenged by his determination*. Jenner's first efforts at publishing his results were rejected. Instead of giving up, he simply went back and got more data until his work was accepted. Vaccination then, as now, was controversial and Jenner had more than his fair share of criticism. Nevertheless, trusting in his knowledge, his studies and his God, he stood firm against his critics.

- Finally, *I'm challenged by Jenner's immunity to fame*. Here is a man who became quite literally a household name across the world, yet his celebrity status left him unchanged. Jenner remained to the end of his life a man who was gentle, humble and gracious.

So at a time when the word *vaccination* is widely heard, spare a thought for Edward Jenner, the man who started it all. A true hero of the faith.

BLAISE PASCAL

The seventeenth-century Frenchman Blaise Pascal in his thirty-nine years of life solved a range of mathematical and geometrical problems, produced a law of hydraulics, achieved breakthroughs in how air pressure and vacuums work, laid the foundations for probability and statistics and planned the first bus network in Paris.

He invented the syringe, the mechanical calculator, the hydraulic lift and the wristwatch. He wrote brilliant essays that are still considered masterpieces of French prose. Yet Pascal not only had a brilliant intellect; underlying everything he did was his Christian faith.

Born in central France in 1623, Pascal was a prodigy who by the age of ten was experimenting in mathematics and science.

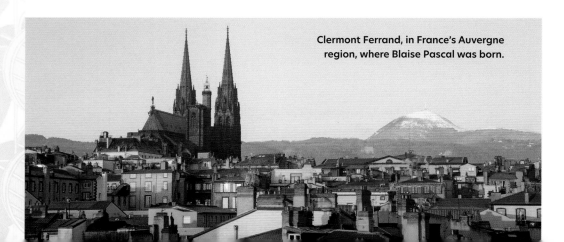

Clermont Ferrand, in France's Auvergne region, where Blaise Pascal was born.

In 1631 his family moved to Paris. Pascal never married but lived supported by his family until his death in Paris in 1662.

Pascal lived in difficult times and was caught up in the big issues of religion and philosophy. One issue arose from the emerging philosophical ideas based on science and reason. For centuries the Christian church had, in effect, said 'just believe'; now, however, they were getting the response 'why?'. Pascal was one of the first people to seriously address the kind of noisy atheism that we hear today.

Night of Fire

Pascal's beliefs acquired a new enthusiasm in 1654 and from then on he became less involved in science and mathematics and more interested in faith and philosophy.

After Pascal's death, a parchment that he had kept hidden in his coat was found. This document – the *Memorial* – is a testimony to what was clearly an overwhelming spiritual event.

Although he died at age 39, Pascal left an incredible legacy as a mathematician, physicist and inventor.

Pascal wrote:

> *In the year of the Lord 1654*
> *Monday, November 23*
> *From about half-past ten in the evening until half-past twelve.*
> *Fire*
> *God of Abraham, God of Isaac, God of Jacob*
> *Not of philosophers nor of the scholars.*
> *Certitude. Certitude. Feeling. Joy, Peace.*
> *God of Jesus Christ,*
> *My God and thy God.*
> *'Thy God shall be my God.'*

This 'Night of Fire' was clearly an overwhelming spiritual experience in which a faith built on reason and ritual encountered the reality of God.

BLAISE PASCAL

Pascal shifted his focus to defending
Christianity and exploring its relationship with
reason. He began to write a book that would
give a reasoned argument for the Christian
faith and wrote a large number of notes, but
before he could put them in order he died.
This work-in-progress, published as the *Pensées*
('Thoughts'), became a Christian classic.

The *Pensées* is full of quotable quotes
that are still relevant today.

On whether reason can bring us to God, we read,
'The heart has its reasons which reason knows nothing of.'

A related thought is,
*'Truth is so obscure in these times, and falsehood so established,
that, unless we love the truth, we cannot know it.'*

In a sentence particularly relevant to our age,
*'The sole cause of man's unhappiness is that he does not know
how to stay quietly in his room.'*

Referring to how we share the gospel,
*'Make religion attractive, make good men
wish it were true, and then show that it is.'*

It is in the *Pensées* that Pascal presents
his 'wager', a famous argument for faith.
Here he wrote that because we all have to
believe whether God exists or doesn't, it is
wisest to gamble on his existence. After
all, if you win, you win everything; if you
lose, you lose nothing. It is an argument
that can be criticised but it makes
the point that the Christian faith is
worthy of careful investigation.

Pascal's tomb is in Église Saint-Étienne-du-Mont, Paris (France).

Pascal challenges me in many ways.

- I'm challenged and encouraged how ***Pascal saw no contradiction between his faith and science***. There is no hint here of the nonsense that you have to make a choice between faith or science. If Pascal could believe in both, so can we.

- I'm challenged by the way ***Pascal defends Christianity***. He saw that reasoned arguments against faith had to be combated by reason. In Pascal lie the roots of the kind of intellectual defence of the faith that we see in people such as C.S. Lewis.

- I'm challenged, too, by the fact that, for all his brilliance, ***Pascal let his faith be shaped by a profound spiritual holy encounter with God***. That 'Night of Fire' transformed him. Pascal loved reason but was prepared to recognise that God can speak to us in ways that go beyond all arguments.

The calculating machine designed by Pascal when he was just 19 years old.

- Finally, I'm challenged by ***all that Pascal did in his short life***. Blaise Pascal demonstrated the truth of the saying that 'it's not the years of a life that count, it's the life in those years'. Let's make the most of the time we are given and let us pray we all have a 'Night of Fire' and be ignited with a holy passion and purpose.

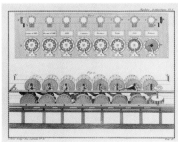

SHI MEIYU

Shi Meiyu was born in Jiujiang, on the shores of China's Yangtze River in 1873. Both her parents were first-generation Christians: her father a Methodist pastor and her mother principal of a Christian school.

For millennia, women had had a well-defined, second-class role in Chinese culture. Of the many injustices girls faced, the worst was that it was still the custom for a young girl's feet to be bound, crushing the bones in order to produce small feet that were the hallmark of a superior social class. In a decision that foreshadowed their daughter's own radical actions, her parents refused to do this.

Jiujiang on the shores of the Yangtze River where Shi Meiyu was born.

Mocked for her unbound feet, Shi Meiyu grew up as an outsider and her father, impressed by a western female doctor, decided that she should train in medicine. Taught in both Chinese and English, Shi Meiyu was sent to the United States in 1892 for professional medical training. Faced with a widespread inability to pronounce her name, Shi Meiyu adopted the name 'Mary Stone' and in 1896 she and a friend became the first Chinese women to graduate as western-trained doctors.

Shi Meiyu returned to Jiujiang and almost immediately demonstrated her independence by politely rejecting a mission board's offer of work in an American-run hospital. Still only twenty-four, Shi Meiyu was confident that it was time for Chinese Christians to take the lead and with a colleague set up a clinic. It was a success and with American financial support she was soon able to open a ninty-five-bed hospital.

A mission hospital in south China in the early 20th century.

Transforming Communities

Shi Meiyu spent nearly fifty years working in China. Despite the fact that her small stature meant that she had to sit on a stool to operate, she became a respected surgeon. She dispensed medicines and carried out tiring medical visits in the countryside, where she would often treat fifty patients in a day. Yet Shi Meiyu was far more than just a pioneering doctor and for years was not only the administrator of the hospital but created and ran training programmes for nurses. Her vision knew no limits and she was involved in setting up hospitals, training centres and schools across China, a nation almost the size of Europe.

Shi Meiyu became a well-known champion for a range of social causes. She did all she could to lift women out of their subordinate status, encouraging some to become doctors, campaigning against foot-binding (which was eventually outlawed) and letting her hospital and nursing school become a haven for abused women. She cared for the disabled, was concerned about orphans – adopting four with a friend – and was one of the founders of the Chinese Red Cross. She continued to maintain good links with the United States, where she was a popular speaker, and after the Second World War she retired there, dying in 1954 at the age of eighty-one.

Meiyu and a number of Chinese nurses.

At the heart of this remarkable woman and her innumerable initiatives was a vibrant Christian faith. In the hospital, the day opened with worship – often led by Shi Meiyu – and she expected her nurses to be evangelists. As an increasing number of young Chinese doctors arrived, Shi Meiyu was able to step back from practising medicine to spend more time on her evangelistic and church work. She was an important figure in the Chinese church, where she is still honoured, and became the nation's first ordained female pastor.

There is much in the life of Shi Meiyu that challenges and encourages me.

- First, I see a *godly passion*. The world is divided into those who are driven and those who drift. Shi Meiyu is in the first category, seeing the spiritual and physical needs of an enormous nation and working tirelessly to meet those needs. It's a great thing to dream dreams but it's an even greater thing to work to make them happen. Do we have her passion and zeal? If not, why not?

- Second, I see a *godly wisdom*. It would have been easy for Shi Meiyu to have burned herself out in the innumerable battles she faced as a doctor and administrator. But she knew her limits and, aware that she could not realise her vision for China alone, trained others in medicine, nursing and evangelism. Most importantly for the long term, she trained them to train others. Equally, Shi Meiyu didn't just campaign for progress,

Pasadena, where Meiyu retired after the Second World War.

she demonstrated by example that Chinese women were capable of the highest levels of skill, learning and administration. Shi Meiyu saw, too, that ultimately China could only be effectively evangelised by the Chinese themselves and had a vision for a truly indigenous church independent of foreign missions. That emphasis was to prove invaluable when the communist government expelled foreign missionaries in 1949.

● Third, I see a *godly balance*. During Shi Meiyu's lifetime China underwent cultural and economic changes that in many western countries had taken centuries. Living through such turbulent times she fought many battles as a reformer. It would have been easy for her extraordinary energies to have been so diverted but her prayerful relationship with Christ remained at the centre of all she was. She was never anything other than a Christian with a heart of Christ.

The Bible reminds us that any genuine living faith must be worked out in practice. In Shi Meiyu's life we see an example of this on a grand scale: she impacted a vast nation for Christ. May the Lord raise up more Shi Meiyus for a time such as this.

LORD SHAFTESBURY

During an age where we topple statues rather than erect them, one man who we can only respect is Anthony Ashley-Cooper, 7th Earl of Shaftesbury. In six decades of public service, Lord Shaftesbury, as he is most conveniently termed, fought successfully against an enormous range of injustices.

Lord Shaftesbury was born into the English aristocracy in 1801. He endured a cold, loveless childhood but found comfort in the love and care of a family housekeeper who shared her Christian faith with him. It's a wonderful example of how seeds sown with children can bear long-term fruit. As Lord Shaftesbury progressed through public school to Oxford University his faith grew and with it an increasing burden for those at the bottom of the social ladder. In his mid-twenties Lord Shaftesbury was elected as a Conservative Member of Parliament and with this was a very public commitment to Christ that motivated everything he did.

In 1827 Parliament appointed him to examine the plight of the 'insane' who were being shut away in 'madhouses'. Here, Lord

Harrow School where Lord Shaftesbury studied 1813–1816.

Shaftesbury showed all the hallmarks of his many subsequent campaigns. He investigated personally and carefully, had compassion on those locked away, considered prayerfully the issues and then framed legislation which, with reasoned, factual and devastating arguments, he drove through Parliament.

In an extraordinary career of fifty years in Parliament, Lord Shaftesbury pursued many causes. He brought forward legislation to outlaw children working in industry, to prevent the employment of women and children down coal mines, to end the appalling practice of using small boys as chimney sweeps, and to tackle the evil of the opium trade. In the absence of a national school system, Lord Shaftesbury promoted the 'ragged schools' to educate the poor.

An example of a ragged school promoted by Lord Shaftesbury.

The Politician

Although these initiatives may seem self-evidently good to us, they were not so at the time: Lord Shaftesbury frequently found himself opposed by those who found his proposals harmful to the economy. A man who was not just godly but also wise, Lord Shaftesbury backed up his Parliamentary initiatives by helping and creating voluntary organisations to generate grassroots support. Significantly, although Lord Shaftesbury was respected in Parliament, he never held a Cabinet office. He was always inclined to put his conscience before the party leadership.

Had Lord Shaftesbury just done this then he would be one of the most remarkable politicians of his century. In fact, it was only part of his life. A committed evangelical Anglican, Lord Shaftesbury involved

The Shaftesbury Memorial Fountain in Piccadilly, London.

himself with many organisations, frequently as president or patron, including the Bible Society, the Church Missionary Society and the Evangelical Alliance. He held strong views about the Second Coming and this gave him an enormous enthusiasm for evangelism amongst Jews. He was particularly wise in identifying where the changes of the Industrial Revolution had produced new challenges for Christian ministry. Here he helped create the Church Pastoral Aid Society, London City Mission and the YMCA, as well as legislation to allow Christian meetings in halls and theatres.

The Nation Changer

Lord Shaftesbury died at the age of eighty-four and was mourned across the nation. Because of his achievements a grateful nation accorded him a statue after his death: the figure that dominates Piccadilly Circus in London (officially 'the Angel of Christian Charity').

Lord Shaftesbury was an extraordinary man. How did he manage to achieve what he did? He certainly had many natural gifts, including a good education, enormous stamina, an ability for public speaking and a privileged status which allowed him to access influential people. Yet he used those gifts wisely. What transformed them was his deep faith, his dedication to prayer and Bible reading and his supportive network of Christian friends.

Three particular distinctives in Lord Shaftesbury's life speak strongly to me.

- First, I see an **astonishing perseverance**. He worked non-stop for the well-being of others for sixty years. He persevered in his campaigns; for instance, he worked to help the mentally ill for over fifty years. He rarely gave up.

- Second, I see an **appealing perspective**. Lord Shaftesbury recognised that his privileged status brought with it a responsibility to those beneath him. Yet beyond this sense of social duty was his permanent awareness that one day he would stand before God. As one of God's children he knew that he had work and duties to do. Politics was not a job for him, it was his calling.

Lord Shaftesbury in 1876.

- Finally, I see an **awesome passion**. Lord Shaftesbury was a man whose heart was grieved by injustice and his indignation drove his social action. Early on in his life, Lord Shaftesbury said, 'I want to be a friend to the friendless.' I doubt there is any briefer or better motive for Christian social action.

Many of the battles that Lord Shaftesbury fought are now history. In the United Kingdom there are no women miners or child chimney sweeps, but other injustices remain.

Let me leave you with a passage from Lord Shaftesbury's diary for Christmas Day 1843 that captures the man perfectly.

'Rose before six to prayer and meditation. Ah, blessed God, how many in the mills and factories have risen at four, on this day even, to toil and suffering.'

It challenges me and I hope it challenges you. May we see a new generation of 'Shaftesburys' rise up for a time such as this.

The House of Commons During a Debate (1858) by Martin Lindsay (1947).

SOJOURNER TRUTH

The woman who became known as Sojourner Truth was born Isabella Baumfree in New York in 1797. Born into slavery, Isabella was to be a slave for thirty years.

She suffered bitterly: her brothers and sisters were sold off in her infancy, she grew up without education and remained illiterate. At the age of nine Isabella was sold at auction with a flock of sheep for $100. Speaking only a form of Dutch, she failed to understand the orders of her new English-speaking owner and as a result was whipped so brutally that she bore the scars all her life. Isabella was to be bought and sold four times by a succession of owners, some of whom abused her physically and sexually. She married another slave with whom she had five children.

Although New York State began abolishing slavery in 1799 it was a task that took another thirty years to complete. In 1826 Isabella, who had some Christian teaching, felt led through prayer to leave her owner. She took an infant daughter but as her other children were still legally bound as slaves she was forced to leave them behind. Free, Isabella learned that her five-year-old son had been sold illegally and took the case to court and recovered her son, becoming the first black woman to win a case against a white person.

Sojourner Truth was whipped so brutally by her owner that she bore the scars all her life.

'Ain't I a woman?'

SOJOURNER TRUTH

In 1828 Isabella moved to New York where she worked as a housekeeper and, becoming involved in various churches, started to acquire a reputation as a preacher.

Isabella's faith grew, and aware that Jesus had liberated her from all that slavery had inflicted on her, she realised that she was indeed 'born again'. As a symbol of that transformation she changed her name to Sojourner Truth on Pentecost Sunday 1843. Her name was chosen because she felt that the Holy Spirit was calling her to become a travelling preacher who would stay only temporarily in places – sojourning – in order to preach the truth. With a new confidence and determination, she travelled across the United States preaching the gospel and that slavery must be abolished. It was not easy: while slavery had been abolished in these regions, discrimination persisted and she was frequently criticised and attacked.

When Sojourner Truth escaped slavery, she found her way to the village of New Paltz in New York State.

Speaker, Evangelist, Reformer

Sojourner Truth soon acquired the reputation of being a remarkable speaker. Nearly six-foot tall, she spoke with poise and passion. She was gifted with words, used vivid imagery, had a ready wit and often accompanied her preaching with song. She was a powerful evangelist but increasingly spoke about social reform, whether slavery, women's rights or prison conditions. Even when she preached on social issues, her love of Jesus and of the Bible (which she constantly had read to her) was always a part of what she said.

Although the name would be considered racist today, The '4th United States Colored Infantry Regiment' was an African-American unit that defended Washington D.C. during the American Civil War.

In 1850 Sojourner Truth gave an account of her life in *The Narrative of Sojourner Truth: A Northern Slave*. An honest account of her sufferings, it sold well and encouraged the growing anti-slavery movement. A year later Sojourner Truth attended a women's convention where she made a passionate speech demanding justice for both women and blacks. Although it made an impact then, it acquired a new life when years later, amid the Civil War, it reappeared in a dramatically rewritten version in which Sojourner Truth spoke in a way that made her sound like a stereotypical black slave of the southern United States. In this popular version, Sojourner punctuates her speech four times with a cry that has gone down in history: 'Ain't I a woman?'

A Continuing Legacy

When the Civil War broke out in 1861, Sojourner Truth helped recruit black troops for the army. She continued preaching and speaking nationally and, an increasingly well-known figure, eventually met President Lincoln.

Sojourner Truth continued her speaking ministry after the war; there were always injustices to denounce and causes to promote. She maintained her speaking ministry until she was well into her seventies. She died in 1883 and her last words were: 'Be a follower of the Lord Jesus!'

Far from being forgotten after her death, Sojourner Truth became an inspiration for subsequent generations. In 2009 she became the first African-American woman to have a statue in the US Capitol and, in an extraordinary gesture, NASA gave her name 'Sojourner' to its Mars Pathfinder robotic rover in 1996.

NASA's Mars Pathfinder mission launched aboard a Delta II booster.

Sojourner Truth impresses in many ways. Let me list just two.

- First, I find myself inspired by her *forgiveness and grace*. Despite having suffered extraordinary injustices, Sojourner Truth forgave and, while continuing to fight against injustice, rejected bitterness. In a speech she admitted that although she had once hated white people, since meeting 'her final master' Jesus, she was filled with love for everyone.

- Second, I'm struck by *how Christ changed her*. Remember, this was an illiterate woman who had been crushed under slavery for the first thirty years of her life. Yet after her conversion, she became someone full of confidence and a sense of mission who preached boldly before thousands. It's a proof that as an evangelist I see everywhere: Jesus Christ transforms lives.

Sojourner Truth was an extraordinary woman with a remarkable sense of mission. She reminds us of what a single life, even with the most unpromising beginning, can achieve. It's something to inspire us all.

A poster announcing a slave sale.

JOHANN SEBASTIAN BACH

Johann Sebastian Bach was born in 1685, and was part of a remarkable German musical dynasty. His world was shaped by the theology of Martin Luther, a great church reformer but also a man who saw music as a gift of God.

Steeped in music from birth, Bach progressively mastered techniques and instruments until he became a composer and church music director. He also studied theology and in his Bible, still preserved, we can see his careful annotations. After a number of short-lived appointments he found a home in Leipzig where for thirty years he controlled music, not just for the churches but also the court and society. He died in 1750 leaving behind an unparalleled legacy of music.

Leipzig, Germany.

Of Bach the man, we know little outside his music. The sparse correspondence we have preserved from him is typical of church musicians of every age and denomination: he defends his music, grumbles over standards and pleads for more resources. We know that Bach suffered many tragedies. He was orphaned as a child, returned from a trip away to find his beloved wife not only dead but buried, and twelve of his children died in childhood. When Bach's music touches on sorrow, you know he's been there.

Bach's music is awesome in terms of both quantity and quality. Quantity? Well, if you want a complete collection of everything he wrote – orchestral, keyboard, cello, violin, flute and the vast body of church music. Quality? Bach had an effortless technical mastery of every intricacy of music. Yet although he was capable of writing works of dazzling mathematical complexity, the music is to be enjoyed and not simply a show of academic brilliance.

Johann-Sebastian-Bach-Kirche, known in English as Bach Church in Arnstadt, Germany where Bach held his first position as organist in 1703, aged 18.

Church Music

Approximately three quarters of Bach's music was written for the church. In the Lutheran church of his day, services (which could be up to four-hours long!) had a substantial musical composition – a cantata – in the middle. For soloists, often a choir and a range of instruments, the cantata was usually around twenty-minutes long; it reflected on the Bible reading and prepared the congregation for the sermon. The church calendar required cantatas for seventy occasions a year and, in one of the greatest sustained feats of creativity in history, for three years Bach created a new cantata every week.

JOHANN SEBASTIAN BACH

Bach playing the clavichord.

This meant that each week he had to set a German text to music (often writing parts for a dozen soloists and players), have the scores copied, rehearse the work and, finally, direct it on the Sunday. Despite the obvious temptation, Bach rarely repeated himself and consistently generated fresh music of extraordinary impact and beauty.

But it was Bach's faith that drove so much of his work. In some ways Bach can be seen as a theologian and preacher who communicated through music. In writing a church piece Bach frequently began with the abbreviated prayer *J. J.* ('Jesus help') and ended with *S.D.G.* (*Soli Deo Gloria* – 'To God alone be glory'). Bach wrote that 'the aim and final end of all music should be none other than the glory of God and the refreshment of the soul', and his intention to praise God and encourage his hearers is there throughout his music.

Of the many things that can be said about Bach, let me mention three I particularly appreciate.

• First, I'm impressed by how ***Bach saw his work as worship***. Yes, church music paid his wages but even when he was writing compositions every week there is no evidence that he was ever 'just doing his job'. He worked for God and God deserved his best. Many of us face the draining burden of having to do things repeatedly. May we stay as fresh and inspired as Bach.

St Nicholas Church in Leipzig where several of Bach's works premiered.

- Second, my heart is warmed by **Bach's profound Christian faith**. The fact is that Bach, following Luther, understood the heart of the gospel to be about how sinful men and women are made right with a holy God through Christ's death on the cross. We, too, must never lose sight of this truth.

- Finally, as an evangelist I am encouraged by the way that in his church music Bach doesn't simply **describe the truth**, he preaches it. He invites a response, seeking to draw his hearers from being merely spectators of the truth into being those who can claim the truth as their own. Over the years Bach's music has proved to be very dangerous for atheists.

In his final years Bach created a work that was meant to be his testament to the world; the B Minor Mass. Unusually, Bach chose a Latin text, probably so that his work might go out beyond Germany and into the world. The final chorus *Dona nobis pacem* is a prayer for God to grant us his peace. It is indeed for 'the glory of God and for the refreshment of the soul'.

J.S. Bach: Sonata for Violin Solo No.1 in G Minor, BWV 1001, first movement *Adagio*.

C.S. LEWIS

I am one of many people who have found both wisdom and wit from the writings of C.S. Lewis. Clive Staples Lewis - known always as 'Jack' to his friends - was born in Northern Ireland in 1898 and grew up in a house overflowing with books.

He was sent to England to be educated where he left his family's formal Christianity to become a professing atheist. After a time on the frontline during the First World War, he began an academic career in English Language at Oxford University which was, in effect, to last all his life. Even when he was made a professor at Cambridge, Lewis still returned to Oxford for weekends.

Magdalene College, Cambridge, where between 1954-1963, C.S. Lewis held the chair in Mediaeval and Renaissance Literature.

'I believe in Christianity as I believe that the sun has risen: not only because I see it, but because by it I see everything else.'

C.S. LEWIS

As a young man Lewis found himself increasingly unhappy with his atheism. With a vivid imagination enriched by extensive reading, he found himself longing for something more satisfying than anything atheism could offer. Conversations about God with many Christian friends, including J.R.R. Tolkien, gradually convinced him that religion could be true and, in 1929, Lewis became a reluctant believer in God, moving within months to a full acceptance of Christianity.

Addison's Walk at Magdalene College, where Lewis, Tolkien and Dyson had a late-night conversation which played a significant role in Lewis's journey of faith.

Without neglecting his increasingly acclaimed academic career, Lewis started defending and promoting his new-found faith. The result was a wide variety of books which were all brilliantly written, well-argued and thoroughly accessible.

Lewis the Author

The Second World War brought him more attention when he became a popular radio speaker; his talks on the Christian faith were published as *Mere Christianity*, a book widely considered a spiritual classic. Lewis wrote many other books on subjects that he knew people found difficult: miracles, pain, prayer and other issues. He also wrote a range of fiction, all of which involved his faith: *The Screwtape Letters*, a science fiction trilogy and the seven children's books of *The Chronicles of Narnia*. Lewis's success came at a cost: his outspoken defence of the Christian faith was resented by his colleagues.

C.S. Lewis Square, Belfast (Northern Ireland).

Lewis's social circle in Oxford was almost entirely masculine but, to everyone's surprise (including his), in his late fifties he found himself in an unlikely romance with Joy Davidman, an American writer. Their happy marriage lasted four years before her passing from cancer. Lewis himself died in 1963 but his books continue to have an extraordinary influence within Christianity and beyond.

C.S. LEWIS

Lewis enjoyed wandering in this local nature reserve while writing *The Chronicles of Narnia.*

Many books have been written about Lewis as a theologian, a writer and a defender of Christianity. Here are some of my favourite C.S. Lewis quotes.

'I think that if God forgives us we must forgive ourselves. Otherwise it is almost like setting up ourselves as a higher tribunal than Him.'

From a devil's point of view: 'The safest road to Hell is the gradual one – the gentle slope, soft underfoot, without sudden turnings, without milestones, without signposts.'

'All that is not eternal is eternally out of date.'

As an evangelist, what I most appreciate about Lewis is the superb way in which he communicated Christian truth. Somehow, he was able to hold together a number of virtues.

- First, Lewis communicated with both ***depth and simplicity***. For a man who lived the cloistered life of an Oxford academic, Lewis was profoundly sensitive to the concerns and struggles of ordinary people. At a time when theologians were discussing questions no one was asking in language no one could understand, Lewis spoke simply and directly to everybody. He had the gift of taking profound and complex theological ideas and, with memorable phrases and relevant illustrations, transforming them into truths that everybody could understand. With his extraordinary knowledge and profound intelligence Lewis could easily have talked down to his readers, yet he had the ability – and the humility – to put himself alongside them. There's a lesson there.

- Second, Lewis communicated to both ***imagination and intellect***. Lewis's personal road to faith had begun with his imagination. He never forgot that and even in his most reasoned works we find him using sparkling language and evocative imagery.

Left: This lion-like carving in a door at Brasenose College, Oxford, is said to have inspired *The Lion, the Witch, and the Wardrobe.*

Magdalen College, Oxford, where Lewis was elected a Fellow and Tutor in English Literature from 1925-1954.

That appeal to the imagination is even stronger in his fiction. Yet at the same time, Lewis knew that appeals to the emotions alone can be dishonest and unhelpful unless they are based on reason. Much of the power of Lewis's writing lies in this simultaneous appeal to head and heart: persuasive claims delivered in gripping prose. There is good sense here. A faith based only on emotions can fail in a time of testing, while one based only on reason can leave the heart barren. Another lesson.

• Finally, Lewis communicated with both *focus and breadth*. Lewis was a bold defender of the Christian faith but he was selective in what he defended. So, he was outspoken on the fundamentals of the faith as the deity of Christ, the truth of the gospels and certainty of heaven: essentials that he famously termed 'Mere Christianity'. Yet beyond such matters he refused to be drawn. There is no agreement on who originally said, 'In essentials unity, in non-essentials liberty, and in all things charity,' but Lewis would have agreed with it. I find there is another lesson there.

Lewis speaks powerfully to those on the edge of faith. Yet he also speaks to us Christian believers who are in need of encouragement and direction. C.S. Lewis is a truly outstanding hero of the faith.

ELIZABETH FRY

The story of how a middle-class lady was able to reform the appalling conditions under which prisoners were treated in Britain and in many other countries, is a classic example of the way God can use unlikely people to extraordinary effect.

Elizabeth Fry was born Elizabeth Gurney in 1780 to a Norwich Quaker family whose Christian faith and traditions were to shape her life. Quakers preferred to dress in a style of plain clothing that made them instantly recognisable. They rejected violence in any form and believed everybody was equal before God and tried to ignore social rank. Unusually for that time, they believed that there should be equality between the sexes so that women often took leadership roles.

At the age of seventeen Elizabeth had a conversion experience and, ever after, was a woman who was committed to public and private prayer, to Bible reading and preaching, and to doing good to others.

Earlham Hall, Fry's childhood family home.

Elizabeth was an anxious child who often suffered from ill health, a trait that persisted through her life. At the age of twenty she married Joseph Fry, with whom she was to have eleven children. Largely because of her husband's support, Elizabeth's childbearing did not get in the way of her social work.

Prisons

In 1813 Elizabeth visited the women's section of London's notorious Newgate Prison and was horrified. The section – built for sixty but now containing 300 – was crowded with women and children who wore rags, slept on straw and suffered every kind of abuse. Quietly outraged, Elizabeth returned the next day with food and clothing, but crises in the family delayed her full involvement in prison work until 1816. Helped by others, she began regular visiting, bringing in food, clothes and books. She created a prison school and began schemes in which inmates could do work and learn skills. She read the Bible to the women and, with considerable effect, preached to them. Seeking to give inmates dignity and self-respect, she involved them in decision making.

Fry in Newgate Prison.

Reform

Realising that the prison system was badly flawed, Elizabeth began to promote the idea that prisons should not simply be places of punishment but also of rehabilitation. She created a number of associations for prison reform in Britain and soon her increasingly popular ideas spread across Europe and the United States.

Gifted with intelligence, charm and a persuasive and persistent personality, Elizabeth campaigned endlessly for change.

Port Arthur, a historic convict site in Tasmania, Australia.

She encouraged prisons to adopt an ethos of kindness and sympathy, to recruit female officers and to protect women by separating them from men. She wrote pamphlets and books and spoke to parliamentary committees. The press made her a public figure and she acquired the nickname 'the angel of the prisons'. Elizabeth used her growing reputation and authority to promote her cause.

The Angel of the Prisons

Elizabeth seems to have been tireless. She was outraged by the transportation of prisoners to Australia, something which exposed women in particular to humiliation and danger. While working for its abolition, Elizabeth tried to minimise the harm of transportation, visiting over a hundred ships and thousands of prisoners. She fought against the excessive use of capital punishment, worked against homelessness and opened a training school for nurses.

Elizabeth Fry died in 1845 but her work continued and she became an inspiration for future generations.

What challenges me about Elizabeth Fry is not just her Christian compassion but the quality of it.

- First, it was a *sacrificial compassion*. It's easy to praise social action at a dinner party or on social media but Elizabeth was someone who was compassionate. With her background she would have struggled with everything about a prison: the squalor,

the smell, the disease. Yet, echoing the Christ she loved and followed, she told prisoners, 'I am come to serve you, if you will allow me,' and service always means sacrifice. She paid a price, too, with the public, some of whom felt that she was reducing the deterrent effect of prisons.

The Convict Brick Trail in Campbell Town. Each brick details a convict's name, their crimes and subsequent punishment.

- Second, it was a **sensitive compassion**. Elizabeth recognised the danger of being condescending and humiliating to those in need. In speaking to prisoners she rarely said '*you*' but would say '*us*'. She stood alongside those who had been abandoned by society and treated them with dignity and respect.

- Third, it was a **sensible compassion**. Elizabeth's compassion was realistic and practical. She encouraged the education and training of inmates so that they could take up a trade when they were released. She made sure that every woman who was to be transported was given a kit that included not only a Bible but also essentials such as sewing equipment. She set up support facilities to assist women when they left prison.

- Finally, it was a **strategic compassion**. Elizabeth knew that what she could do alone was limited. She used her personality, her social links and her influence to get others involved with her. The results were that her labour outlived her.

Elizabeth Fry's compassion is challenging. She recognised there was a scandal in the prisons and, becoming indignant, did something about it. There are no shortages of scandals today but I find myself wondering where is *our* indignation? Where is *our* compassion? May the example of Elizabeth Fry inspire us today to do 'good works'.

The Convict Ship c. 1820 by Henry Adlard.

97

REMBRANDT

The great seventeenth-century Dutch artist Rembrandt is an unusual Christian hero, yet, by universal agreement, he is one of the truly great Christian artists.

Rembrandt Harmenszoon van Rijn was born in 1606 in the Dutch town of Leyden. He grew up immersed in the Bible, which was to shape his art.

As a teenager Rembrandt demonstrated remarkable artistic talent. He began a career as a painter of portraits and quickly acquired a reputation for producing portraits that saw beyond the physical features to the character beneath. He was also gifted in drawings where he was able to capture lives and landscapes.

In 1634 Rembrandt married Saskia van Uylenburgh. Despite the deaths of three of their four children in infancy, Rembrandt continued to develop his skills in painting. Commissioned to paint a formal portrait of a group of wealthy volunteers, he produced the awesome *The Night Watch*, a painting of extraordinary realism that broke every convention.

The Night Watch (Dutch: *De Nachtwacht*) by Rembrandt (1642).

In 1642 everything changed. Tragically, Saskia died after her fourth pregnancy and Rembrandt's habit of letting expenditure exceed income began to catch up with him. Saskia had left him an income but only if he didn't marry anybody else. Possibly as a result, Rembrandt found himself in a disastrous relationship which ended up in the law courts and incurred displeasure from church and society. He then had a longer, happier marriage with a woman named Hendrickje Stoffels.

By now, however, Rembrandt's style was falling out of fashion as people preferred more elegant, dramatic portraits. Refusing to compromise, Rembrandt continued to produce works of art, often of landscapes and biblical themes. Rembrandt no longer simply portrayed biblical scenes; he let the Bible speak.

The Rembrandt House Museum in Amsterdam, the Netherlands.

Rembrandt's Later Years

In 1657 poverty forced Rembrandt to auction most of his prized possessions and move to a more modest house. Hendrickje died in 1663 and Rembrandt died in 1669, leaving behind a daughter and hundreds of his paintings and drawings. Buried as a poor man, his extraordinary talent was only recognised much later.

REMBRANDT

A reconstruction of one of the rooms in Rembrandt's house.

What encourages me about Rembrandt? It is not simply his artistic brilliance; it is that in his artistry I find things that, as an evangelist, I admire.

- First, ***Rembrandt shows us the value of humanity***. Rembrandt had a fascination with human beings. In everyone he painted or drew – including himself – we see an honest fascination with who they are as *people*. Everybody, whether they are a major or minor figure in his pictures, is depicted with authenticity and affection. People counted to Rembrandt and, in an age when human beings are reduced to elements on a spreadsheet or items on a database, he reminds us that every single one of us is valuable because we are made in the image of God.

- Second, ***Rembrandt shows us the nature of humanity***. One of Rembrandt's characteristic techniques was to paint faces half in light and half in darkness. In doing this

A self-portrait (1669).

it seems to me that Rembrandt takes a biblical view of who we human beings are. On the one hand, we are made in the image of God, yet we are all people on whom the shadow of sin has fallen. Rembrandt's artistry shows human beings as they really are: beautiful but flawed.

- Third, **Rembrandt shows us the Bible story**. Rembrandt was a deeply biblical artist with a third of his work based on the Bible. For Rembrandt the Bible was the story of reality; of real events happening to very real people. To add to the authenticity of his Bible images, Rembrandt consulted Jewish rabbis. That the Bible was not just history but also personally relevant is highlighted by the way that Rembrandt often portrayed himself as a character, even in crucifixion scenes. One of his most remarkable images is 'The Hundred Guilder Print', a scene that seems to portray the whole of Matthew chapter 19.

The Return of the Prodigal Son, one of Rembrandt's final masterpieces, c. 1669.

- Finally, **Rembrandt shows us grace**. Rembrandt applied the Bible to himself. One of his last paintings is *The Return of the Prodigal Son* in which we see the younger son of Luke 15 being welcomed back home by his father who, in a gesture of reconciliation and acceptance, has lovingly put both his hands on him. The son has come home. It's a story that Rembrandt clearly identified with; his turbulent life revealed that he seek and receive grace from Jesus our Saviour. But then whose life does not?

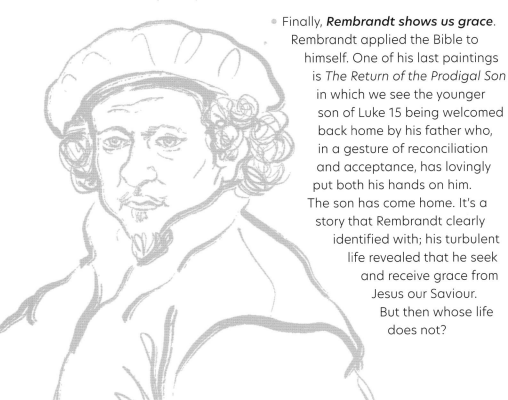

JOHN STOTT

The great Christian leader John Stott, is a man who helped and encouraged so many people across the world, including me.

John Stott was born in 1921 in London. He was naturally gifted, possessing a brilliant mind, an amazing memory and an extraordinary self-discipline. John was brought to a living faith in Christ at public school through the preaching of Eric Nash, and applied himself to his new faith with great commitment.

At Cambridge, where he studied modern languages, John became deeply involved with the Christian Union. He trained as an Anglican minister before becoming a curate at All Souls Langham Place, London, the church he had attended as a child.

Throughout his ministry John remained based at All Souls: he spent thirty years there as curate and rector and then for over thirty years was based there as a writer, preacher and leader. John's passion for evangelism transformed All Souls and it became a focus for evangelical ministry in London and beyond. One notable emphasis of John's preaching from the start was the way that he didn't simply preach the historic gospel but also the need for Christians to apply it in their daily lives.

Stott studied modern languages at Cambridge University.

John had many talents and his ministry and influence soon spread beyond central London. Always having a strong interest in student evangelism, John preached at university missions across the world for a quarter of a century. He wrote extensively, producing Bible commentaries, practical guides to Christian living and also important texts on how Christians should relate to the world.

A Scholar

He wrote over fifty books and many articles, all distinguished by his scholarship, precise language, a solid biblical basis and a contemporary application. His books were translated into many languages, the profits from which were used to support theological education across the world. Three books in particular have proved to be of enormous impact: *Basic Christianity*, which has led many to faith, *The Cross of Christ* on the atonement (one of my favourites) and *Issues Facing Christians Today* which encourages Christians to engage effectively with the world in which they live.

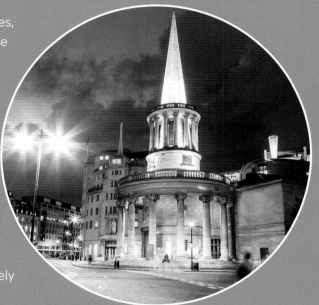

All Souls, Langham Place.

A Statesman

With time John became a national and international Christian statesman with a powerful if gracious influence. In his own Anglican church he played a major role in turning evangelicalism from being a minority belief to a mainstream element. Internationally, he planned meetings and chaired committees including those for the important Lausanne Covenant (1974). Either by quiet counsel or open support John was involved with an extraordinary range of evangelical initiatives such as the London Institute for Contemporary Christianity, the conservation organisation A Rocha, Tearfund, the Evangelical Literature Trust and many others.

JOHN STOTT

Stott retired from public ministry in 2007 and moved to Lingfield, Surrey. He died 4 years later aged 90.

John's ministry was truly global: he visited over a hundred countries speaking, preaching and encouraging and, where possible, taking the opportunity to enjoy one of his pleasures – birdwatching. He continued with his international ministry well into his eighties until, with his health fading, he retired from ministry. He died in 2011 at the age of ninety.

John was able to do so much and was helped by his own astonishing self-discipline, by Frances Whitehead (his formidable and protective secretary) and by his purchase of a rundown cliff-edge cottage in Wales – The Hookses – where he could retreat, pray and write in peace. He also saw his singleness as something that freed him to serve the church more fully.

A Personal Reflection

I was privileged to meet with 'Uncle John' on many occasions. I was particularly encouraged when, still finding my feet as an evangelist, he invited me to tea, supported what I was doing and encouraged me to deepen my knowledge of God through Bible reading and prayer. One cherished memory is how, whenever I met him, he would give me a characteristic hug, gaze at me with his blue eyes and ask, 'Brother John, are you still preaching the gospel?' to which he would inevitably add, 'This is the one thing you *must* do!'

One of the fascinating and challenging things about John was the way that he balanced things that could have easily been opposites.

• So although John was ***extraordinarily self-disciplined*** he was also *gentle*. He would rise early at five or six o'clock in the morning and devote himself to prayer and Bible reading. He seemed to live life with a remarkable efficiency and never seemed to waste time. Yet there was never any sense of him being any sort of driven individual whose projects demand priority; with John you always felt that people came first.

• Equally, although John was an ***authority***, he was also ***humble***. He was one of the very few Christian leaders to be known and respected globally: *Time* magazine labelled him as one of its '100 Most Influential People' in 2005. Yet you never felt any sense of superiority or self-importance with John: he listened graciously to other views and always seemed to have time for people. He lived humbly too; it's fascinating that the only property he ever owned was that tiny cottage in Pembrokeshire. With John, the idea of being a servant of others was no cliché but the truth.

• Finally, although John was a ***deeply spiritual man***, he was also ***utterly relevant***. He was a man who let prayer and Bible reading shape everything he said, did and was. Yet there was no sense of him being any sort of religious mystic, too holy to deal with the mess of the world. With John there was always this desire to be involved: he was a man who wanted to change the world for God.

John Stott was a remarkable man. Like many people, I look around at the Christian world today and wish that we had his wisdom and authority to guide us. But as I think that, I can hear John's voice in gentle rebuke, reminding me that the hope of Christ's church lies not in its leaders, but in Christ himself.

CHARLES H. SPURGEON

Charles Haddon Spurgeon was undoubtedly the greatest preacher of nineteenth-century Britain.

He was astonishingly prolific: he preached thousands of sermons, almost all of which were printed and circulated worldwide so that, at his death, some 56 million copies had been printed in nearly forty languages. Yet Spurgeon's achievement was not simply one of quantity. He was a godly man who preached God's truth in a way that was serious and challenging yet overflowed with warmth, passion, wit and humour. Spurgeon's profound spiritual insight was often expressed in memorable sayings. Two of my favourites are: *'A Bible that's falling apart usually belongs to someone who isn't'* and *'The greatest joy of a Christian is to give joy to Christ.'*

The Wheatsheaf Inn in the village of Kelvedon, birthplace of Charles Haddon Spurgeon.

Spurgeon was born in Essex in 1834 into a Christian family. He had only a very basic education but throughout his life made up for it by constantly reading books. Although growing up amongst committed Christians, Spurgeon only came to a personal faith in Christ at fifteen. From then his growth to Christian maturity was meteoric and, aged only nineteen, he was called to be the minister of a London Baptist church. Within months Spurgeon's attractive preaching was filling the church and, as word spread, he was forced to move to successively larger venues. Finally, in 1861 Spurgeon acquired a purpose-built church, the Metropolitan Tabernacle, with seating for 5,000 people, and there he stayed for the remaining thirty-eight years of his life. He preached regularly to extraordinary numbers – once to 24,000 people at Crystal Palace – and without any amplification.

Marriage and Illness

In 1856 Spurgeon married Susannah Thompson, a woman who was to be an extraordinary source of support and strength to him. Both their lives, however, were blighted by illness: Susannah became an invalid and Spurgeon struggled throughout his life with depression and other ailments. As the years went on he took to spending the winter months at Menton on the French Côte d'Azur where he worked on writing sermons and publications, dying there in 1892 at the early age of fifty-seven.

Spurgeon was such a uniquely talented individual that it is hard to do him justice. He was gifted with intelligence, stamina, memory, a remarkable voice and a wonderful way with words, all of which he nurtured through reading, prayer and fellowship with godly people. He was astonishingly energetic – he often worked eighteen hours a day – something that doubtless helped him to his early grave. He was a man of both generosity and discernment in what he believed. Although a convinced Baptist himself, he had friends across denominations and rarely took sides on what he saw were unimportant differences in belief. Nevertheless, when it came to the

Engraving of Spurgeon preaching his 'Humiliation Day' sermon at The Crystal Palace, 7th October 1857.

essentials of the gospel he stood firm, and in bitter battles that took their toll, he fought long and hard for the historic faith.

Sayings and Doings

Spurgeon has been called the 'Prince of Preachers' yet his deep commitment to social action mustn't be overlooked. As he himself said, 'When our biographies shall come to be written, God grant that they may not be all sayings, but sayings and doings!' He created and led several organisations, including those which trained theological students and helped church planters, as well as others which worked amongst the orphans, widows and prostitutes. He fought evil wherever he found it; for example he thundered against slavery to such an extent that his books were burnt in the United States.

Because Spurgeon was such a unique man at such a unique time, to seek to imitate him is either impossible or dangerous. Few of us have his voice, his memory or his energy. We can, though, all seek his love of Christ and the Bible and his zeal to spread the gospel. As an evangelist, however, there are four specific things that inspire me.

• There was *appeal* in his preaching. Spurgeon lived when many preachers preferred polite, comfortable discourses on morality to the challenge of calling people to turn to Christ. In contrast, Spurgeon proclaimed the gospel with a passionate expectation of seeing men and women brought to faith. He preached not for praise, but for a verdict.

• There was *authority* in his preaching. In Spurgeon's day there was a great pressure to modify the gospel in the interests of 'progress'. Spurgeon would have nothing of this, standing firm with a confident authority that

Left: Spurgeon preaching at the Surrey Music Hall.

The Metropolitan Tabernacle in Elephant and Castle (London).

came from his trust in the Bible as God's unbreakable Word ('The Bible is like a lion. You don't have to defend it. You just have to let it loose') and Christ as the very heart of its message ('Whatever subject I preach, I do not stop until I reach the Saviour, the Lord Jesus, for in him are all things').

● There was an *authenticity* in his preaching. Spurgeon spurned the contemporary trend for polished pulpit speeches delivered with formality and calm dignity. Instead, he preached with boundless energy, wit, warmth and, above all, *life*. In his preaching he was himself a sinner who had been redeemed by grace and who overflowed with his joyful knowledge of Christ.

● There was *accessibility* in his preaching. Spurgeon had grown up amongst country folk and in London never neglected those who lacked education. He spoke to his hearers in simple words that they would understand and respond to. He used anecdotes and wit to grip them while he hammered in the truth. Spurgeon was widely sneered at as being vulgar, theatrical and undignified yet he drew and held his hearers, moving them through both laughter and tears to transformed lives.

Spurgeon spoke with spiritual power and life to his generation. By the grace of God may we do the same to ours!

LILIAS TROTTER

The remarkable story of Lilias Trotter, artist and missionary, deserves to be much better known.

Born into a privileged family in London in 1853, Lilias became a believer in Christ in her teens and was soon involved in Christian movements that encouraged her to seek a deeper spiritual life. Wealthy enough not to need to earn a living, Lilias began working as a volunteer in London with working girls by day and with prostitutes at night.

Lilias had an extraordinary gift for art. At the age of twenty-three, when staying in Venice with her mother, they found that the famous art critic and philosopher John Ruskin was in the same hotel. Boldly, Lilias's mother asked if Ruskin would look at her daughter's work. The great man reluctantly agreed, only to find himself captivated by what he saw. Ruskin, whose friendship with Lilias was to last until his death in 1900, began tutoring her as an artist.

Grand Canal, Venice.

Eventually he challenged her by saying that if she would give herself fully to art she could become the 'greatest living painter and do things that would be Immortal'. It was an incredible offer given that Ruskin had successfully launched the careers of other artists. Lilias agonised in prayer before deciding that her art must take second place: she had to 'seek first the kingdom of God and his righteousness'.

Missionary Work

Lilias continued with her charitable and evangelistic work in London but in 1884 she underwent surgery which left her with a weakened heart. Despite this she felt called to missionary work in North Africa and applied to two organisations, only to be rejected because of her poor health. Undaunted, she and two other single women simply went to Algeria on their own.

Trotter arrived in Algiers, Algeria, in 1888.

So with poor health, no knowledge of Arabic and without support from any organisation, Lilias began her ministry as a missionary. At first she and her colleagues were based in Algiers but as the work expanded and she was joined by other workers, they mounted extraordinary expeditions deep into the Sahara across a vast area from Morocco into Tunisia.

Severe Opposition

Lilias faced constant challenges. She was a single woman in a very masculine culture and her health remained so frail that she frequently had to return to Europe to convalesce. She was opposed, not just by those who rejected her preaching, but also by the French colonial government. Furthermore, although she and her colleagues saw conversions to Christ, there were discouragements as many converts came under appalling pressures to renounce their faith.

© AWM

Nevertheless, Lilias persisted, and as the years passed the mission work expanded and little fellowships of Christian believers grew. Eventually, in her seventies, Lilias became confined to bed where she spent her time in prayer, writing, painting and managing the mission. She died in Algeria in 1928 after four decades of labour, grieved over by both her colleagues and by many Algerians to whom she had shown God's love.

Innovation and Legacy

Lilias was an innovative missionary. She decided to work with women and children, doing what we today would call 'coffee bar evangelism', using music and producing attractive leaflets (she used her artistic gifts well) in easy-to-understand colloquial Arabic. A typical example was how Lilias was able to use the mystical and experiential side of her faith to reach out to mystics in the Sufi branch of Islam and to speak to them of the only answer to their search for God: Jesus.

Lilias's labours were fruitful. Despite persecution and the emigration of believers, the Algerian church has endured and her mission organisation continues today as Arab World Ministries. No less significant is the fact that her mission practices have been adopted across the world.

Let me mention three features of the life of Lilias Trotter that I find inspiring.

- First, Lilias was a **woman of vision**. As an artist she had an extraordinary ability to see the natural world, and as a Christian she was gifted with a similarly profound spiritual perception, something

that she nurtured by seeking God daily through Bible reading, prayer and meditation. Her gift of insight helped her see what was right both for her life and for her efforts for the gospel. In both the physical and spiritual sense Lilias was a woman always looking towards the horizon. Would that there were more like her.

• Second, Lilias was a *woman of decision*. Faced with the overwhelming complexity of modern life many people find that it's easier just to drift and let things happen. In contrast, Lilias was a woman who could – and did – make decisions. Given the extraordinary offer of becoming a famous artist she carefully and prayerfully chose to do something more. In North Africa, faced with endless challenges for herself and for those who worked with her, she proved to be a leader who made wise and strategic choices.

Trotter's tutor art critic John Ruskin.

• Third, Lilias was a *woman of determination*. In her spiritual life, she rejected any superficial knowledge of God but instead hungered to know him better. Diagnosed with lasting health problems it would have been perfectly sensible for her to remain in London, but instead she chose to go to Algeria. Even there she would delight in leaving the relative comfort and security of the capital to visit remote and dangerous regions. Lilias was a woman who, having decided what she had to do, did it.

Ruskin had promised Lilias that if she would give everything to her art she could do things that 'would be Immortal'. She rejected that offer, but we can be confident that what she achieved for Christ instead will last for eternity.

113

MICHAEL FARADAY

The extraordinary life of Michael Faraday, perhaps the greatest scientist of the nineteenth century, reads like one of Charles Dickens' novels.

Faraday was born in 1791 into an impoverished family in what is now Southwark, London. His father was a blacksmith and Faraday's education was basic. The family, however, was supported by their church. Throughout his life Faraday kept up his involvement with his church and gave a clear testimony to a personal relationship with Christ.

At the age of eleven, poverty forced Faraday into work. He began running errands for George Riebau, a French bookbinder, who, recognising Faraday's potential, took him on as an apprentice. Faraday began to read and Riebau wisely directed him towards useful books. He soon became fascinated by science. The bookbinder encouraged Faraday, gave him space to conduct his own experiments and eventually enabled him to hear lectures by the world-famous chemist Humphry Davy.

Inspired by Davy's talks, Faraday wrote to the chemist and soon became his assistant at the Royal Institution, a body that specialised in applied science. Davy found the

Faraday's home at 2 Blandford Street, during his apprenticeship to George Riebau.

young man remarkably useful and took him on an eighteen-month tour of Europe, visiting many of the great scientists of the time.

On his return to England, Faraday continued to help Davy but increasingly began to do his own experiments in chemistry and, later, physics. Faraday turned out to be a superb experimental scientist. He was imaginative and methodical and tried to test for himself every scientific claim he came across. He was a hard worker and rapidly published his discoveries, writing nearly 500 papers in his long career.

International Success

Step by step Faraday rose to the very highest levels of international science. He became the director of the Royal Institution, was awarded a doctorate by Oxford University and made a fellow of the prestigious Royal Society – indeed he was twice invited to become its president but refused because he wanted to continue his laboratory work. Despite his honours, Faraday remained humble, lived on a modest salary and refused a knighthood, preferring to be 'plain Mr Faraday'. He did, however, accept an apartment at Hampton Court given to him by the monarch, along with a small pension.

Hampton Court Palace.

Faraday worked hard – possibly too hard because eventually his health failed – but he was sustained by two things. The first was his marriage in 1821 to Sarah Barnard with whom he had a long and happy, if childless, partnership. The second was his deep Christian commitment and his church involvement: he was not only a faithful church member, elder and preacher, but also regularly involved in visiting the poor and sick.

Faraday's achievement is even more remarkable when we consider that the odds were stacked against him. He remained something of an outsider in society; he was lower class and had almost no formal education. However, he was accepted not just because of his brilliance as a scientist but because of the way his gentle, humble manner won him friends.

Faraday's study at the Royal Institution.

The 'Patron Saint of Electricity'

In the early 1840s Faraday's health began to deteriorate. Typically, when it was proposed to him that he would be buried in Westminster Abbey along with monarchs and scientists such as Isaac Newton, he refused. He died in 1867 at Hampton Court.

In his prolific career Faraday's studies covered a vast area. He has been referred to as the 'Patron Saint of Electricity' and much of today's world relies on principles he first discovered – the dynamo, the transformer, the electric motor, electrolysis and so on – but Faraday's expertise was much wider. He invented the process we use in refrigeration, recognised the potential of ether as an anaesthetic and discovered the important chemical benzene. The list of discoveries goes on.

Faraday's ascent from being an absolute nobody to a very considerable somebody is definitely inspiring. I am particularly challenged by three things.

- Faraday was committed to *seeking* truth. A particular Christian emphasis in Faraday's thinking was the way that he saw the natural world as something created and governed by a God who had given rules which human beings could, and should, follow. Inspired by a vision that everything in nature was ultimately connected, he peered forward into the future, anticipating ideas that were to be developed by Einstein (who had a portrait of Faraday in his office to inspire him).

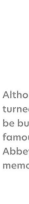

Although Faraday had turned down an offer to be buried in London's famous Westminster Abbey, he does have a memorial plaque there.

- Faraday was committed to **sharing** truth. Scientists can be notoriously bad at communication but Faraday, doubtless remembering his own experience, was different and always anxious to publicise what was being done. He himself was a good communicator and full of enthusiasm. He arranged accessible public lectures, including some for children, a tradition continued today as the Royal Institution Christmas Lectures.

- Faraday was committed to **serving** truth. There was no gap between what he believed and what he did. In his role as the nation's 'chief scientist' Faraday served society: investigating mine explosions, working on better lighthouse lamps, preventing the corrosion of ships, and raising issues about industrial and water pollution. Faraday didn't just do good, he also resisted evil, refusing to develop chemical weapons for use in the Crimean War.

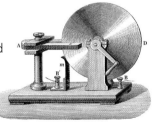

The Faraday Disk, the first electric generator.

Michael Faraday's life is full of towering achievements. To do all that he did, against the odds, and maintain his Christian witness is astonishing. You don't have to be Einstein to find him an inspiration!

GEORGE WASHINGTON CARVER

To understand George Washington Carver, the great African-American agriculturalist and educator, you have to know something of the world in which he lived. Even though slavery was legally abolished across the United States in 1865, it cast a long-lasting and bitter shadow. African-Americans now lived in freedom, but poverty and discrimination continued.

Carver was born in Missouri in 1864 and named simply 'George' by the Carver family, who owned his parents. George's father died before George was born and, when a week old, the boy and his mother were kidnapped. The Carvers were able to ransom George, but no trace of his mother was ever found. In a rare reflection on his past, the adult Carver was later to say he started life as 'the orphaned child of a despised race'.

Now raised by the Carvers as one of their children, George suffered many illnesses, and instead of doing manual labour, developed interests in nature and gardening. Because there were no local state schools for black children, Carver decided to attend one ten miles away. There, a kind woman gave him

The home of the Carver family who initially owned George before raising him as one of their own children.

accommodation and encouraged him to drop the slave name 'Carver's George' for George Carver. (He was to add the 'Washington' later.)

As an African-American, Carver found it hard to get anything beyond a basic education. He went to Kansas, only to be refused entry to a college because of his race. He moved to Iowa where he studied art, and his teacher, noting how well he painted plants, encouraged him to study botany. In 1891 Carver became the first black person to attend what is now Iowa State University and earn a degree. He continued studying crops and their diseases, gaining respect as a botanist and eventually becoming the first black lecturer there.

George Washington Carver, probably at Tuskegee.

Innovation and Peanuts

Carver's abilities came to the attention of the famous Booker T. Washington, the principal of Tuskegee Institute, Alabama, the first college of higher education for black people. Carver was invited to teach agriculture and, feeling called to serve his own community, accepted. He was to stay at Tuskegee for forty-seven years until his death.

Carver became aware that his teaching and research had to be appropriate for the mainly black poor farmers around him. A major problem was that farming was based on cotton, a crop which rapidly impoverished the soil. Carver, doing research with the most basic equipment, began to develop and teach improved farming practices. He promoted crop rotation using alternatives to cotton, such as sweet potatoes, peanuts and soybeans, in order both to restore the soil and to improve the livelihoods of the impoverished farmers. He

Peanuts dug up and turned over for drying in preparation for harvest.

Peanut specimen collected by Carver.

taught appropriate skills: the feeding of pigs with acorns instead of expensive commercial feed and the enrichment of the soil with swamp mud instead of fertilisers. He developed a touring laboratory and classroom that travelled around analysing soils and teaching better practices.

One result of Carver's emphasis on crop rotation was a surplus of peanuts. In order to improve the market for these, Carver ingenuously created new products such as peanut milk and found uses for peanuts in cooking, salads, oil, paper, cosmetics, soaps and other products. His advocacy of the peanut brought him national recognition. In the 1920s and 1930s, Carver – 'The 'Peanut Man' – was a national celebrity and became widely consulted by presidents and others on matters of agriculture, particularly for the poor south. He stayed active until his death at the age of seventy-eight in 1943.

A Living and Practical Faith

Carver the man remains something of an enigma. He was a quiet, introspective individual who lived frugally and dressed shabbily. He was hard-working, humble and soft-spoken, and although he lived at a time when racial injustice persisted, he rarely showed anger about it. Although he lived on the Tuskegee campus he was a private man, and he never married.

At the heart of George Washington Carver was his faith. He spoke of his conversion at the age of ten, was a churchgoer all his life and taught Bible studies for thirty years. He emphasised Christian morality in his teaching and practised it in his life; he liked to pray to God as Creator out in the woods. Yet Carver's faith was profoundly practical, and he frequently claimed that his insights came from God.

The creek at George Washington Carver National Monument.

Three aspects of the life of George Washington Carver strike me.

● First, Carver's life was one of **generous involvement**. With his ingenuity and ability Carver could have escaped the poor south. There are stories, for example, that the inventor Thomas Edison offered Carver a high-salary job. Yet Carver stayed where he felt called to and served his people. Where are we called to?

● Second, Carver's life was one of **gentle inspiration**. He became a role model for African-Americans, quietly inspiring a generation that needed encouragement by demonstrating what they could do. His enthusiastic teaching inspired generations of students to improve the lives of poor farmers. Carver left a powerful legacy: what will ours be?

Arachis hypogaea, more commonly known as the peanut.

● Third, Carver's life showed **godly insight**. Carver's open statements that he sought guidance from God and heard his answers were often quietly ridiculed. Such scorn seemed justified when, after Carver's death, many of the agricultural practices he promoted were replaced by 'big agriculture' with its mechanisation, enormous fields and extensive use of fertilisers and pesticides. Yet in recent decades, as the problems with this type of farming have become obvious, there has been an increasing call for precisely the sort of sustainable agriculture that Carver taught, with farmers working with the land rather than against it. Once known as a man who spoke for the poor African-American communities of the southern United States, Carver is now seen as an environmental prophet of global relevance. Why don't we listen to God more often?

GLADYS AYLWARD

When I became a Christian in 1975 my spiritual diet was Bible reading and Christian biographies. One life that impacted me was that of Gladys Aylward, a remarkable missionary to China from 1932 to 1949.

Gladys was born in north London in 1902 to a working-class family and had only limited education. She was a small woman, only four foot ten inches in height, with a Cockney accent. She worked as a housemaid and, after becoming a Christian, was seized by a desire to share the gospel in China.

She applied to the China Inland Mission and was accepted on a three-month course to assess her suitability. She was rejected on the grounds that she would be unlikely to learn the difficult Chinese language and unable to manage and cope with life in the Far East. Disappointed, Gladys returned to domestic service but her vision for China continued to prompt her. Eventually, she heard of an elderly lady missionary in China who needed a companion. But how was she to get there? She had no organisation to support her and didn't have the money for the boat fare.

The former China Inland Mission headquarters in Newington Green, London, where Aylward likely studied her initial three-month course.

So in 1932, Gladys simply decided to go to China by train. She went across Europe and joined the Trans-Siberian Express which took her towards Vladivostok. It was a hazardous journey and at its eastern end she found herself caught up in fighting between Russia and China. Finally, after five and a half weeks and surviving all sorts of hazards, she reached her destination of Yangcheng in central China.

The Trans-Siberian Railway.

The 'Virtuous One'

Staying with this elderly missionary, Gladys immersed herself in the language and culture and adopted local dress. Confounding the verdict previously delivered on her, Gladys became fluent in Chinese. An old inn was rented and named The Inn of the Eight Happinesses after the eight noble values: love, virtue, gentleness, tolerance, loyalty, truth, beauty and devotion. The inn provided an outstanding opportunity for sharing the gospel, and over the next few years Gladys led many people to Christ.

The local authorities approved of Gladys and when the government outlawed the traditional practice of binding the feet of young girls, she was appointed an official inspector to check the law was being obeyed. She demanded – and received – the right to tell the women and girls about Jesus in the course of her work. She was even called to intervene in a murderous prison uprising and not only quelled the riot but was able to get improved conditions for the prisoners. Gladys soon found herself caring for a growing number of orphans. Her efforts at helping people earned her the name 'Ai-weh-deh' which means 'Virtuous One'.

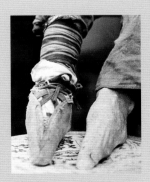

Bound feet in the early 1900s.

By 1937 China had become involved in a complicated and bloody three-way conflict between the government, communist insurgents under Mao Tse Tung and an invading Japanese army. Wanting to identify with those she served, Gladys abandoned her British nationality and became a Chinese citizen. After a Japanese advance

she found herself behind enemy lines; she reported information to the Chinese authorities, an action that eventually led to her being on a Japanese 'Wanted' poster.

The war worsened and Gladys was injured in a bombing raid. Realising that her orphans needed to be taken away from the fighting, she led more than a hundred children in an epic trek over the mountains to safety. When, after twenty-seven days, Gladys finally delivered the children to an orphanage beyond the war zone, she collapsed with typhus and malnutrition.

England, Hong Kong and Taiwan

Although Gladys made a recovery and continued her work and witness in other parts of China, her health was affected by what she had undergone and in 1949 she returned to England. Although she wanted to go back to China the new communist government was opposed to Christianity, making the return impossible. Gladys remained based in England, preaching widely, before eventually going to British-administered Hong Kong and finally settling in Taiwan. There she founded the Gladys Aylward Orphanage with which she worked until her death in 1970.

Gladys's remarkable story became the subject of a book, *The Small Woman*, by Alan Burgess. It was a bestseller and was turned into a film, *The Inn of the Sixth Happiness*, which was released in 1958. The film annoyed Gladys because it took

The Inn of the Sixth Happiness (1958).

enormous liberties with her story, not least in having her portrayed by the tall, blonde, Swedish actress Ingrid Bergman. Ironically, however, it raised the profile of both Gladys and, more to her liking, the gospel she preached.

The life of Gladys Aylward is full of virtues: courage, compassion and an extraordinary determination. Three things strike me.

- First, Gladys Aylward is a ***challenge to the complacent***. She had a lifelong and unquenchable hunger to see men and women on the other side of the world come to Jesus. Where are her successors today? The church desperately needs people with her passion and zeal for people and the gospel.

- Second, Gladys Aylward is an example of ***faith to the hesitant***. She didn't simply believe something about God, she had a faith that motivated her to face challenges and overcome obstacles. I find myself wishing for more examples of such Spirit-inspired faithful determination that will attempt and achieve great things for God.

- Third, Gladys Aylward is an ***encouragement to the discouraged***. Gladys was a little woman who viewed herself as being ordinary. Nevertheless, she put her trust in God and he used her in an extraordinary way. She faced a succession of obstacles, yet in Christ she overcame them all.

Throughout her Christian life Gladys relied on Philippians 4:13:

'I can do all things through Christ who strengthens me.'

She found it true for her; may we find it true for us today.

Chinese symbol for virtue.

APOLO KIVEBULAYA

Some heroes of the faith are forgotten and deserve rediscovery. One of these being Apolo Kivebulaya, a remarkable church worker in Africa for forty years and a reminder of the way so many African Christians have spread Christianity on that continent.

Apolo was born into a peasant family in 1864 in Kampala in what is now Uganda, and given the name 'Waswa'. It was a time when his world was beginning to change dramatically. The extraordinary carving up of the continent by the European powers had begun, and alongside came European missionaries with the gospel.

The first missionary arrived in Uganda in 1877 and Christianity spread rapidly. It soon met opposition and in the middle of the 1880s the king ordered the brutal killings of Christian converts – the famous 'Uganda Martyrs'. Sometime afterwards, Waswa became a Christian, taking the name Apolo after Apollos, the church leader of Acts 18. He was baptised in 1895 and immediately began working with the Anglican Church. He was briefly married but his wife died; deciding that God wanted him to remain single, he chose not to remarry.

Kampala, Uganda,

A man of incredible energy and enthusiasm, Apolo began church planting. Under the leadership of the Church Missionary Society he worked in the foothills of north-western Uganda and, clearly gifted in evangelism, saw numerous conversions and the start of many new congregations. Soon Apolo accepted the challenge to go west to evangelise the tribes in the Belgian-controlled area that is now the Democratic Republic of the Congo, and set off, crossing the snow-capped Rwenzori Mountains in winter. Of the moment when he was finally able to gaze westwards into the heart of Africa he wrote: 'I stood and looked far away to the Congo. The prospect terrified me.' Yet driven by his faith, his courage and his compassion for those who did not know Jesus, he went onward.

Imprisonment

Despite now finding himself in a very different culture, his powerful preaching met with great success. Less popular, however, were his demands, not just for conversion but for a changed lifestyle. Finding an opportunity to expel him, a chief had Apolo escorted back to prison in Uganda. There, greatly discouraged, Apolo had a vision in which Jesus appeared shining like the sun, telling him, 'Take heart, for I am with you.'

Eventually, Apolo was released but the Belgian colonial authorities had closed the border and for twenty years he stayed in Uganda as a church planter. There he travelled hundreds of miles annually on foot (he never wore shoes in his life) and by bicycle. He preached simply, emphasising Jesus and the cross but always

APOLO KIVEBULAYA

Mount Baker, part of the Rwenzori Mountains National Park, 1.7 miles from the border with the Democratic Republic of the Congo.

insisting that converts live out their new faith consistently. He encouraged the translation of the Bible into local languages and was particularly concerned about such social issues as education and the care of infants and deserted women.

In 1903 Apolo was ordained a priest in the Anglican Church and frequently found himself acting – with remarkable grace – as an intermediary between European missionaries and the African congregations.

In 1915 Apolo was able to return to the Congo and began rebuilding the church he had left there. His enthusiasm for evangelism never waned and within a few years he felt called by God to be a missionary to the little-known Pygmy tribes of the deep forest. Despite great differences of culture and language, his personal warmth and grace allowed him to win converts for Jesus and he developed a network of small congregations across many tribes.

Facing West

Finally, Apollo was called back to Kampala where he was made a canon of the cathedral. Told that he had a fatal illness, he requested that, despite the tradition that he should be buried facing eastwards, he would be buried facing the opposite direction, to emphasise that the gospel needed to go to the west. He died in 1933 and his wishes were respected.

Apolo Kivebulaya served God at an extraordinary time. In 1890 there had been just one church with 200 members in Uganda but by 1927 there were 2,000 churches with nearly 185,000 members. The change was not simply in numbers, but the leadership was now increasingly African. Under God some of that explosive growth and development was Apolo's work.

Ugandan flag.

Apolo's missionary passion, persistent joyfulness and saintly life brought praise from everybody. It's an utterly inspiring life and let me mention three aspects of it that challenge me.

- First, Apolo had an **active faith**. His was a life of constant action: preaching, teaching, organising, travelling and praying. All he did was prayed over and wisely chosen. He was also an activist with vision; one of those precious souls who is always looking to the horizon. We could do with more like him today.

- Second, Apolo had an **astute faith**. He lived at a time of political, religious and technological change in which the world he was born into was overturned. In that cultural turbulence Apolo led wisely. So, for instance, he rapidly adapted to that technological innovation of the bicycle and delighted to use it for the gospel. Yet, above all, Apolo simply steered a steady course: preaching the gospel, teaching converts and establishing churches. In similarly turbulent times there's a lesson for us.

- Finally, Apolo had an **authentic faith**. The best evidence for talking about Jesus is to live like him. Every report of Apolo, whether from Europeans or Africans, speaks of how he overflowed with the fruit of the Spirit. He was praised for his love, gentleness, sympathy and sincerity, had the simplest of lifestyles and cared deeply for people, especially the vulnerable. His was not a faith of mere words but of a transformed life that honoured God and won people to Christ.

Apolo Kivebulaya lived in a very different world to ours. Yet his life of faith and service remains relevant and challenging to us all wherever we live.

JAMES CLERK MAXWELL

Let me be honest. When it comes to the physicist James Clerk Maxwell I struggle to understand even a fraction of his achievements. He was undoubtedly one of the very greatest of physicists - Einstein had Maxwell's portrait on his wall to inspire him. In practical terms, Maxwell's insights into the principles of electromagnetism laid the foundation for our modern world: radio, television, smartphones and the Internet.

James Clerk Maxwell was born in 1831 in Edinburgh, Scotland. An extraordinarily curious child, Maxwell investigated everything he could find. He grew up in a deeply Christian home and by the age of eight could recite all 176 verses of Psalm 119! His mother, who had been personally educating him, died when he was eight and Maxwell's later education was first at the Edinburgh Academy and then, from age sixteen, Edinburgh University.

In 1850 Maxwell went to study at Cambridge University. There, he subjected his Christian beliefs to a thorough analysis and, after a conversion experience, took hold of a mature and confident faith that was to endure throughout his life. In 1854 he graduated with a degree in mathematics and began

14 India Street, Maxwell's birthplace in Edinburgh.

a teaching and research career at Cambridge. Rising rapidly in the science world, in 1856 he was appointed professor at Marischal College, Aberdeen at the young age of twenty-five.

In 1857 Maxwell married Katherine Dewar with whom he shared a deep Christian faith. There are many letters to Katherine in which Maxwell discusses Bible passages that he knew they were reading together.

A Famous Discovery

Maxwell applied his intellect and his mathematical skills to many subjects. One of his first successes was to solve the two-centuries-old mystery of the rings of Saturn. In his published analysis – with sixty pages of complex mathematics – he proposed that they must be made of numerous small particles; a conclusion vindicated by space probes. In 1860 he moved to King's College, London, where he worked on colour photography and explored issues to do with electricity and magnetism. In London he became acquainted with the elderly Michael Faraday. Although very different personalities, it can be said that if Faraday dominated the physics of the first half of the nineteenth century, it was Maxwell who did so in the second half.

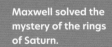

Maxwell solved the mystery of the rings of Saturn.

A Legendary Legacy

He was appointed the first professor of physics at Cambridge in 1871. There he created the Cavendish Laboratory, an institution that was to acquire a legendary reputation as a centre for physics, generating thirty Nobel prizes. Maxwell's personal faith can be seen in the way

The James Clerk Maxwell Telescope at Mauna Kea Observatory, Hawaii (USA).

that he had Psalm 111:2 inscribed on the doors: 'Great are the works of the Lord; they are pondered by all who delight in them.'

In 1879 Maxwell's health failed and at the age of forty-eight he died. The minister who visited him in his last weeks reported that he spent his final days with a faith that was confident in 'the gospel of the Saviour'.

Physics and the Light of the World

Maxwell's greatest achievement was the way that he was able to unite what had been considered to be three separate phenomena: electricity, magnetism and light. His studies laid the basis for the Theory of Relativity and modern physics, and Einstein himself said that 'one scientific epoch ended and another began with James Clerk Maxwell'.

Maxwell openly declared his Christian beliefs and knew his Bible to the extent that it was widely believed that he had memorised a lot of it. His was also an intelligent faith: Maxwell could – and did – discuss theology with bishops. He belonged to an evangelical Presbyterian church and in his later years became a church elder. In terms of his character, he was widely praised for his calmness, humour, generosity and humility.

Parton Church, where Maxwell is buried.

Maxwell is a hero of the faith because he combined his commitment to the Christian faith with the very highest levels of science. Three things strike me.

- First, Maxwell's faith **satisfied** him. Here was one of the most intelligent minds who constantly questioned every aspect of how the universe works. Yet he built his life around a biblical Christianity and remained perfectly content with it. Some people today seem to feel that doubt is a virtue and that a spiritual restlessness is praiseworthy. Not so with Maxwell: he was a man who was committed to his Christian faith.

- Maxwell's faith **stimulated** him. He was cautious about how God's eternal truth linked with the provisional and changing ideas of science. Yet his Christian faith gave him a vital framework for his research. He believed that because the universe had been created by God and that human beings had been made in God's image, it was perfectly reasonable that we could – and should – try to understand the universe.

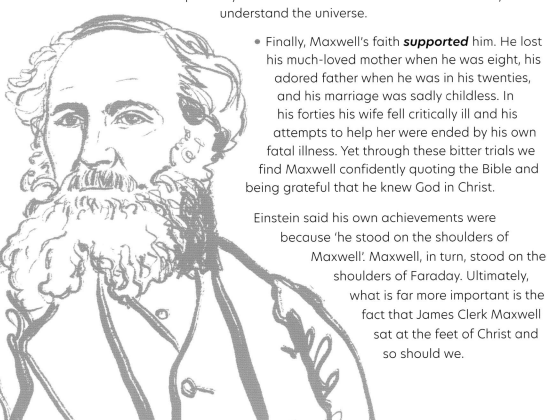

- Finally, Maxwell's faith **supported** him. He lost his much-loved mother when he was eight, his adored father when he was in his twenties, and his marriage was sadly childless. In his forties his wife fell critically ill and his attempts to help her were ended by his own fatal illness. Yet through these bitter trials we find Maxwell confidently quoting the Bible and being grateful that he knew God in Christ.

Einstein said his own achievements were because 'he stood on the shoulders of Maxwell'. Maxwell, in turn, stood on the shoulders of Faraday. Ultimately, what is far more important is the fact that James Clerk Maxwell sat at the feet of Christ and so should we.

WILLIAM HOLMAN HUNT

Although William Holman Hunt is mostly remembered for The Light of the World, *that extraordinary portrait of Christ knocking on the door of the soul, he created many other striking paintings.*

The Light of the World **by** Hunt.

Born in 1827 into a working-class London household, Hunt grew up in an atmosphere where Bible reading was encouraged. He started work as a clerk at the age of twelve but soon entered art school. Acquiring a reputation as a painter, in 1848, along with Dante Gabriel Rossetti and John Everett Millais, he founded the Pre-Raphaelite Brotherhood, seeking a return to the dynamism, colour and detail of mediaeval painters.

Encountering Christ

Hunt soon acquired his own distinctive style, painting in vivid colours with brilliant lighting and extraordinary detail, and with a remarkable commitment to accuracy. As his artistic career started to rise, Hunt began to return from atheism to the Christian faith. Increasingly his paintings carried an open or subtle message. In painting *The Light of the World* in 1851, Hunt felt that, in some way, he had encountered Christ.

A typical Hunt painting of the same time is *The Awakening Conscience* which at first glance seems to be merely a married couple having a disagreement. Looking closer we observe details, including the lack of a wedding ring, which tell us that this is the moment when a man's mistress has suddenly become aware of the possibility of repentance.

The Middle East

Hunt, anxious to achieve accuracy in his biblical paintings, now took the first of four journeys to the Middle East. Like many Victorian travellers he fell in love with the nature of the area and spent seven years there. During his first visit he produced the remarkable *The Scapegoat*, with its forlorn animal alone in the desolation around the Dead Sea. Although referring to the animal of Leviticus 16:22 that carried the sins of God's people into the wilderness, Hunt also saw it as pointing to Christ as the ultimate sin bearer and had Isaiah 53:4 painted on the frame:

'Surely he hath borne our griefs, and carried our sorrows: yet we did esteem him stricken, smitten of God and afflicted.'

The Scapegoat by Hunt.

WILLIAM HOLMAN HUNT

In 1865 Hunt married Fanny Waugh, who sadly died in childbirth on an Italian tour with him the following year. In 1875 Hunt married Fanny's younger sister Edith.

Hunt continued to produce dramatic canvases, often with a spiritual message, and became popular with the public. In our age of high-definition television it's not easy to recapture the impact that his vibrant and detailed paintings must have made at the time. In the art world, however, Hunt fell out of fashion. Impressionism, which deliberately ignored any commitment to detail, had become popular and morality was now something that people wanted to escape from, rather than endorse. Hunt died in 1910 and was buried in St Paul's Cathedral, close to his final version of *The Light of the World*.

Why is Hunt a Christian hero? Without doubt he was a remarkable artist and a Christian, and in many ways an evangelical. Personally, I'm fascinated by the way that he communicates Christian truth.

- First, Hunt's paintings are **compelling**. It's hard to ignore a Holman Hunt painting: with few exceptions, they immediately catch the eye. We are drawn in by their colours, detail and dynamism. His first audiences, used to 'religious art', were engaged (and in some cases enraged!) by what they saw. So in *The Shadow of Death* we have Jesus as a bare-chested carpenter in his workshop, stretching his tired arms wide, and his mother Mary has her back to us. For some people the realism and authenticity were just too much.

The Shadow of Death by Hunt.

- Second, Hunt's paintings are **challenging**. One of the sad features of much art of all kinds is that many artists, however skilful, ultimately have nothing to say. That's never the case with Holman Hunt: almost all

St Paul's Cathedral in London, where Hunt is buried.

of his paintings convey a message, whether subtle or obvious. Equally challenging is the sense of authenticity and realism found in his paintings. As in *The Finding of the Saviour in the Temple* or *The Shadow of Death*, Hunt constantly reminds us that the biblical story is not a fairy tale but real-life accounts of people who existed and events which happened.

● Third, Hunt's paintings are **convicting**. Many of Hunt's canvases can be considered to be 'sermons in paint'. One of the dismissive comments about him is that he was a 'moralist'. Well, living as we do at a time where there is a deficit in morality I find that something more to be praised than condemned. Many of his paintings are about conversion in some form or another and often he seems to be sounding a warning. So, for instance, in *The Hireling Shepherd* we have a shepherd who is preoccupied with an attractive country girl, while in the background the sheep are straying and in danger. It's all about Jesus' reference in John 10:11-15 to the 'hired hand' who, not being the shepherd, doesn't care for the sheep. There's a powerful warning in it to all in any position of church responsibility: don't be distracted, care for the flock.

Hunt's art was compelling, challenging and convicting. Isn't that what our preaching about Christ should be?

WILLIAM CAREY

If you've ever wondered how much anyone can do in a lifetime then take a look at William Carey.

Born in Northamptonshire in 1761, the young Carey soon showed extraordinary linguistic ability. Leaving school at fourteen he became a cobbler, but as he worked on shoes he studied new languages. He came to faith in Christ in his teens and, at the age of twenty, married Dorothy.

In 1783 Carey was appointed a local schoolmaster. His mind, however, was increasingly focused on more distant horizons: he researched all he could to find out about the world and the extent of Christianity, praying over the vast areas where the gospel had not been preached.

Carey House, an eighteenth-century grade II listed building where the Baptist Missionary Society was founded in 1792.

In 1792 Carey printed a pamphlet entitled *An Enquiry into the Obligations of Christians to use Means for the Conversion of the Heathens*, arguing that Jesus' Great Commission of Matthew 28:16-20 was still binding on the church. Shortly afterwards he preached a sermon to Baptist leaders, out of which came a phrase that was to be permanently associated with him: 'Expect great things from God; attempt great things for God.'

A painting of ships arriving into Calcutta in 1792. Carey arrived in Calcutta in 1793.

The result was the creation of what was to become the Baptist Missionary Society and it was soon agreed that he personally should go to India. In 1793 Carey, with a pregnant wife and four children, set sail on a journey that was to take five months. For the first few years in India they faced not just poverty and ill-health but the hostility of the British colonial authorities to missionary activity. Finally, Carey got a job managing a dye plant that allowed him to continue translating the Bible into the Bengali language.

Translation and the Printing Press

Eventually, after seven years of struggle, matters began to improve. There was the first trickle of converts and, after relocating to a Danish colony at Serampore, now part of greater Calcutta (Kolkata), Carey was able to set up the printing press from which came the first Scriptures and textbooks in local languages. Two missionaries, Joshua Marshman and William Ward, also arrived and, with Carey, formed a powerful team that endured for decades. In 1801 the British authorities recognised Carey's extraordinary ability by offering him a position teaching Bengali at a college for British civil servants. This position allowed Carey to translate the Bible into other Indian languages.

Gate where Carey preached. Dhaka, Bangladesh.

Setbacks, however, continued. Dorothy Carey died in 1807. (Carey was to suffer the loss of his second wife and to remarry a third time.) There were countless illnesses, the deaths of colleagues and children and a fire that destroyed years of work. Yet as time passed, the achievements of Carey and his co-workers accumulated. Between 1801 and 1832 his Serampore Press printed

Serampore College, Serampore. Founded by Carey in 1818.

212,000 copies of books in forty different languages. Forty-five free schools catering for thousands of pupils of every social class were created, and in 1818 Serampore College was founded to train pastors but also to provide education to anyone 'regardless of caste, colour or country'. It was to become the first institution in Asia to grant degrees.

Carey the Pioneer

Carey spent his final years quietly revising his Bengali Bible, preaching and teaching. He died in India in 1834, aged seventy-two.

How much can anyone do in a lifetime? Carey sets a very high benchmark. He mastered numerous Indian languages, translating the Bible into Bengali, Oriya, Assamese, Marathi, Hindi and Sanskrit. In his lifetime, his mission printed and distributed all, or parts, of the Bible in over forty languages and dialects. He pressured the British authorities for wide-ranging social reforms including outlawing widow burning and child sacrifice, and he worked constantly to undermine the caste system. He protected lepers, introduced savings banks to fight crippling interest rates for borrowers, and encouraged education in every form and for everybody, including women, lower-caste individuals and the poor.

*'Expect great things from God;
attempt great things for God'*

WILLAM CAREY

Somehow he found time to study and write extensively on Indian botany and set up the Agricultural Society of India with a view to improving India's farming system. Carey's achievements are even more remarkable precisely because he was a pioneer: he followed in no one's footsteps.

Line engraving from an American artist showing Carey baptising converts.

In considering all that Carey did over four decades in India I'm struck by how he lived out in different ways the three great Christian values of faith, hope and love.

- Carey's *faith had determination*. He saw the world's need to hear the gospel and committed himself to it. In India he pushed on through discouragements, difficulties and disasters. When asked about his achievements Carey said that he was a plodder: 'I can plod. I can persevere in any definite pursuit. To this I owe everything.' I think we could do with a few more plodders today!

- Carey's *hope was seen in his expectation*. Theologically, Carey was an optimist and held the view that God's will was that the kingdom of God would ultimately expand across the world. As such Carey saw his role not simply in seeing short-term effects but in laying the foundations of a glorious church in Asia. In our time, such confidence and long-term vision are much needed.

- Carey's *love was displayed in his compassion*. Carey loved India and his passion for social reform was driven by his desire for men and women to find the freedom that there is in Christ. That compassion was seen in a desire to understand Indian culture. Although Carey never drifted from his belief in Christ as the only Saviour of humankind, he engaged deeply with Indian culture, translating many of the Hindu epics into English. Carey's work is a reminder that all we do must be done in love.

'Expect great things from God; attempt great things for God' was the motto Carey gave to history. Carey did both and in doing so became a man who achieved great things for God. May we also 'expect great things from God' and 'attempt great things for God'.

AMANDA SMITH

The life of Amanda Smith was extraordinary: she travelled from being a black slave to becoming the first international woman evangelist.

Amanda was born in 1837 in the American state of Maryland, the first of thirteen children. Her parents were slaves and she became one too. Despite the poverty of her upbringing Amanda grew up surrounded by prayer and Bible reading and was taught to read and write by her parents. Through hard work, her father managed to buy freedom, first for himself and then for his family.

Although free, Amanda still suffered discrimination and was to have a very limited education. She became a maid at thirteen and was to work as a domestic help until her mid-thirties. She married at the age of seventeen and had two children, only one of whom survived into adulthood. Her husband died in the Civil War.

Smith spent her early life in rural Maryland.

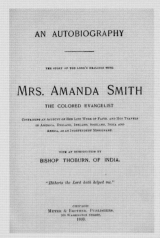

In her early twenties Amanda felt that God had miraculously cured her of a serious illness for a purpose. Shortly afterwards she had a transforming conversion experience. Now a single mother, she married again but sadly her husband, who had misled her over his spiritual ambitions, deserted her. Amanda was left in poverty with three more children, all of whom were to die in infancy.

Increasingly, Amanda became involved in Methodist Church circles and became a well-known evangelist, bringing people to trust in Christ, in churches (whether black or white) and at Christian meetings. She was a powerful speaker: nearly six-foot tall with a rich voice, a remarkable singing gift and an exuberant, dynamic and spontaneous manner. Amanda was a preacher who made an impact; where she spoke people were converted, overcome with repentance or touched with a sense of God's presence.

Living by Faith

In 1869, after the death of her last son and her second husband, Amanda felt called to be a full-time missionary. As a freed black slave, a mere 'washerwoman' as she was often described, and without education or formal training, she could not obtain any sort of official church position. Instead, for the remainder of her life Amanda was to live by faith, sustained by gifts. She certainly acted by faith, rarely planning anything but instead praying over everything and relying on God to guide her.

A camp meeting in the early 1800s.

Amanda began preaching at special events – 'camp meetings' – where large numbers of people gathered for days of church services with an emphasis on conversion and holiness. In 1878 she was invited to cross the Atlantic to speak at the Keswick Convention in England. She soon became a popular speaker at revival meetings throughout Britain. She drew crowds because her preaching reached hearts.

AMANDA SMITH

Amanda was invited to go to India, where for eighteen months she had considerable success in revival meetings. Instead of returning to the United States, she felt led to visit Africa and spent eight years evangelising and setting up schools and missions in Liberia and Sierra Leone.

Racism and Sexism in the 19th Century

When she finally returned to the United States Amanda wrote a long account of her life, with an honest account of her spiritual journey but also an eyewitness account of the problems of racism and sexism faced by a black woman in the nineteenth century.

From 1892 onwards Amanda focused her efforts on helping her own African-American community, in particular by establishing and running an orphanage in Illinois. In her last years, with her health failing, she moved to Florida where she died in 1915 at the age of seventy-eight.

Amanda Smith came from the most unpromising background to be extraordinarily used by God for forty years in evangelism and revival across four continents. Her success was due to God's gifting of her, but she played her part by allowing God to work in her life. Three things strike me about Amanda's life.

Smith served God as an evangelist across four continents.

• First, she **depended upon God**. Amanda was a poor woman with limited education working against widespread racial prejudice. Yet those very limitations forced her to rely on God and on his strength. The life of Amanda Smith is a reminder that God does most through those who count themselves least.

• Second, she had **a desire for God**. The nineteenth-century emphasis and enthusiasm for 'holiness teaching' is unfashionable today. Amanda made it her priority to seek God and to reflect that knowledge and experience of him in her life. It's a good priority to make our own.

• Third, she **demonstrated the grace of God**. Amanda was a woman who suffered. She lost four of her five children, lived a life of poverty and was frequently considered a second-class citizen. Yet hers was a life of remarkable graciousness. She never demanded her rights, accused others or complained about the racism she endured. Although she rarely raised discrimination in public – she did an enormous amount of good by building bridges and demolishing barriers between black and white communities.

Amanda Smith achieved much for God in her generation. She sets an example for us in ours.

JOHN PATON

John Paton was born in 1824 in Scotland, the eldest of eleven children in a poor but devout Christian family.

When he was twelve he had come to a personal faith and committed himself to being a missionary. As a young man Paton moved to Glasgow; there he undertook theological and medical studies, was ordained in the Presbyterian Church and worked for ten years as an evangelist. He then felt called to what was then the New Hebrides, a long island in the south-west Pacific that is now part of Vanuatu and where heroic mission work had been undertaken for some time.

In 1858 Paton sailed for the South Seas, taking with him his bride Mary. What they found when they landed on the island of Tanna horrified them. Poverty and ill-health, brutal clan battles, cannibalism, infanticide and the sacrifice of widows was practised. Brutality against women was so common that old women were rare. In addition, there was an atmosphere of spiritual fear due to the widespread belief in evil spirits and the practice of witchcraft.

Tanna Island, Vanuatu.

Three months after his landing Paton was struck by a double disaster, losing both his wife Mary and his newborn son to disease. In his grief he found himself alone, struggling with a language that had never been written down and under the constant threat of violence from the islanders. Despite being encouraged to return home, Paton continued to serve for four years under difficult circumstances in which he saw very little fruit.

Paton the Mobiliser

When in 1862 large-scale tribal warfare broke out, Paton was forced to leave. He then developed a new role as someone who mobilised the church for mission. For four years Paton travelled around Australia and Scotland talking about the needs of mission. He was an inspiring speaker, telling personal stories and speaking with a challenging authority about the need for personnel and financial support for ministry on the islands.

In 1864 Paton married again and with his new wife, Margaret, returned to the New Hebrides, this time to the island of Aniwa. There they were to labour for decades and to have ten children, four of whom sadly died in infancy. They learnt the local language, wrote it down and translated and printed a New Testament for the islanders.

Paton lived and ministered in the New Hebrides between 1858-1862 and 1864-1881.

Three months after landing on the island of Tanna,
Paton lost his wife and newborn son to disease.

The Patons were also very much involved in practical help: educating, creating employment and starting medical and social care. The impact of both preaching and practising the gospel was remarkable; within two decades the entire island had become practising Christians.

In 1881 ill health forced Paton to give up being resident at Aniwa and he became one of the very first worldwide missions speakers, travelling through Europe, Australia and the United States. His influence was helped by his dramatic autobiography and the nickname given him by the influential preacher C.H. Spurgeon as 'the king of the cannibals'. In his addresses, though, Paton was careful not simply to talk about his own adventures and sufferings but also to tell stories of how violent men had, after turning to Christ, been transformed into gentle human beings.

Paton made three worldwide tours and became involved in political action for the New Hebrides, in particular campaigning against slavery which trapped men from the islands. In between his voyages around the world, he returned to the islands and in 1899 was able to give the Aniwans their complete New Testament. With advancing frailty, Paton and his wife retired to Australia, where Margaret died in 1905 and he followed two years later.

Clearly, John Paton was a man of outstanding faith but what I find challenging is how that faith was worked out.

- Paton's faith gave him *courage*. He faced extraordinary opposition and in his early years as a missionary had to live with death, loneliness, illness and a constant threat of violence.

Left: Spears from the New Hebrides and Fiji.

In particular, after the loss of his first wife and child no one would have blamed him for returning to Britain. Yet he stayed at his post.

● Paton's faith gave him **confidence**. The almost immediate death of his wife and child on Tanna and the seeming failure of his attempts to change a hostile culture for Christ must have seemed strong evidence that he'd been mistaken about God and his calling. Yet Paton persisted through discouragements, believing that God had not only called him but was in control. As Paton was to declare when a precious mission ship was wrecked, 'My blessed Lord Jesus makes no mistakes!'

Royal Navy ship HMS *Fly* in New Hebrides c. 1848.

● Finally, Paton's faith was demonstrated in **commitment**. First, he was a man committed to the gospel. It would have been both easy and understandable for Paton to compromise in his preaching by accepting some of the tribal practices or superstitions. Yet he remained loyal to the historic gospel. He was also committed to his people. Despite living at a time in which many educated individuals considered the peoples of the South Pacific and Australia as subhuman savages incapable of civilisation and destined for extinction or slavery, Paton cared for and valued the islanders. Believing that social reform went hand in hand with the gospel, he and his wife taught the islanders reading and crafts, built orphanages, had schools erected and dispensed medicine. They battled, too, against those outsiders who sought to exploit the islanders by selling weapons and alcohol.

Although our world is changed from that in which Paton lived, God has not changed. Paton wrote,

'God gave his best, his Son, to me; and I give back my best, my all, to him.'

May we also give back our best, our all, to God today.

PANDITA RAMABAI

Pandita Ramabai was a truly extraordinary woman, reformer, educator and evangelist.

She was born in 1858 into British-ruled India that was dominated by the Hindu caste system which placed everybody in rigid social levels and treated women as inferior to men. Her father was a high-caste Hindu priest who, defying tradition, taught both Pandita and her mother to read Sanskrit, the sacred language of the Hindu scriptures.

In the famine of 1876–1878 Ramabai, aged sixteen, lost both parents and a sister to starvation. Penniless, she travelled with her brother over India, publicly reciting the Hindu scriptures. She was gifted with an astonishing memory and was invited to speak before the holy men – the 'pundits' – in Calcutta. They were so astonished with her knowledge of the sacred texts that she was awarded the title *pandita* – 'the learned one'.

Displaying the independence that was to be a life-long characteristic, Pandita broke cultural rules by marrying a man from a different caste. Sadly, her husband soon died, leaving her a widow with a daughter at the age of twenty-three. In Hindu belief, the loss of a husband was felt to be a punishment on the wife for something bad done either in the

Ramabai had an incredible understanding of Sanskrit and the Hindu scriptures.

Ramabai moved to Pune in 1882.

present or in a past life, with the result that widows were condemned to live in exclusion and poverty. Pandita, by now an orphan, a widow and a single mother, found herself in the worst of all situations.

Defiantly rejecting any exclusion, Pandita began creating an association that would promote women's rights – including education, women doctors and an end to child marriage. She soon became a figure to be heard and spoke powerfully in an enquiry run by the British authorities. In various ways, Pandita encountered Christianity and, coming across a copy of Luke's gospel, found herself impressed with how Jesus treated women.

Discovering Christianity

In 1883 Pandita went to Britain with her daughter in the hope of becoming a doctor, a venture that failed due to her advancing deafness. She stayed with an Anglican women's community where she was impressed by their care for prostitutes and the homeless. She decided to become a Christian and was baptised. It was a high-profile conversion that was considered a betrayal back in India. Although Pandita accepted Christianity, she retained much of her culture, wearing Indian dress and remaining vegetarian.

Pandita was passionate about reforms in India and travelled to the United States. There she wrote a book that was very critical of the way women were treated in India. She developed close friendships with many American Christian

Ramabai with her daughter.

women activists, including Harriet Tubman, and gained support from a wide range of churches and organisations. Pandita returned to India in 1888 where she immediately became involved in social work and opened Mukti, a residential centre near Mumbai where young widows could learn to read and write and be secure. It grew rapidly and by 1900 had 1,500 residents.

Discovering Christ

Pandita's life was transformed in 1891 when she read the book *From Death into Life* in which the English vicar William Haslam recounted his dramatic conversion from a dead formal Christianity to a living faith. Pandita wrote,

> *'One thing I knew by this time, that I needed Christ and not merely His religion. I had at last come to an end of myself, and unconditionally surrendered myself to the Saviour.'*

From now on Pandita's life had a new power and joy and although she remained heavily involved in social work, she was now an evangelist, preaching to all a message that focused on Christ, the Holy Spirit and prayer.

Inspired by news of the Welsh revival of 1904 Pandita encouraged prayer for revival in India, and in 1905 there were extraordinary encounters at Mukti as the Holy Spirit fell, giving deep repentance, conversions and profound and lengthy worship. The revival spread out across India and was a tremendous encouragement in the United States when, a year later, the Azusa Street Revival broke out.

Pandita was an extraordinary linguist – she was fluent in seven languages including Greek and Hebrew – and in the last two decades of her life worked to create a new and more accessible Bible translation in her own Marathi language. It was finally completed just days before her death in 1922 at the age of sixty-four.

Pandita had a remarkable life and three things intrigue me about it.

Stri Dharma Niti (Morals for Women) written by Ramabai in 1882.

- First, ***the progress of Pandita's faith is fascinating***. Ramabai starts off as a good person – a committed social activist – who makes a Christian commitment and is baptised but who, some years later, comes into a deeper, joyful, Spirit-empowered faith. It's easy to get stuck in a rut in the Christian life and I suspect a lot of us need to progress from where we are.

- Second, ***the passion of Pandita's faith is inspiring***. Ramabai always had an enormous passion to change things for the better. With her first 'head commitment' to Christ and her later 'heart surrender', that zeal grew, deepened and became more focused. Here's a quote about Pandita late in her life: 'She has but one idea, one ideal, and that is that she may reflect the Lord Jesus Christ. Pandita Ramabai radiates the Lord Jesus.' We need more like her!

- Third, ***the price of Pandita's faith is challenging***. She lived sacrificially, earning nothing and owning nothing. She paid a price elsewhere. With her independence and challenging faith, Pandita found herself something of an outsider, not just with Hindus but even with churches and missions in India.

Although Pandita Ramabai was called by one Indian academic 'one of the greatest Indians in all history' she has been largely forgotten by her nation. I think it's time to remember her.

HUDSON TAYLOR

Hudson Taylor was not just an extraordinary missionary to China, but an incredible example of a life fully surrendered to God.

James Hudson Taylor was born in 1832 in Yorkshire, England. He grew up in a Christian family, started work in his father's pharmacy when a teenager and, after a period of rebellion, was firmly converted at the age of seventeen.

China

Taylor took his relationship with God seriously and China soon became his passion and priority. It was a daunting task. The journey to China took five months by a hazardous sea voyage which had a reputation for inflicting illness on visitors. Undeterred, Taylor began preparing himself by learning Mandarin and acquiring medical training. Above all, he learnt to be dependent on God.

At the age of twenty-one Taylor sailed for China as the first missionary of the newly formed Chinese Evangelisation Society. Arriving in Shanghai in 1854 he found the city in turmoil but soon began preaching in the region. Realising that his western clothes and hairstyle created an unnecessary barrier to the gospel, he boldly dressed in Chinese clothes and a hairstyle with a pigtail.

Aged 19, Taylor moved to Kingston upon Hull to be a medical assistant to Dr Hardey in preparation for a life of service.

In 1858 Taylor married Maria Dyer who helped train women workers. Poor health troubled the family and soon Taylor fell ill. In 1860, with every expectation that Taylor would not be able to come back to China, they returned to England. Here, however, he not only recovered but finished a Bible translation, gained medical qualifications and wrote a book on the needs of China.

Maria Jane Taylor.

China Inland Mission

Taylor also gained a growing reputation as a powerful speaker on China. In 1865 he founded his own organisation, the China Inland Mission (today's OMF). It was innovative in being non-denominational, offered no guaranteed income and relied entirely on God for provision. Other distinctives soon emerged: a vision for a Chinese church led by Chinese, and the recruitment of ordinary people and single women as missionaries.

In 1866 Taylor took his family and a party of sixteen missionaries back to China. Arriving at a time of renewed instability they began moving deep into the interior of China, preaching and distributing Bible portions.

Zhujiajiao Ancient Water Town, a historic village in the Qingpu District of Shanghai.

In 1866 Taylor took his family and a party of sixteen missionaries back to China.

Ill-health continued to take its toll on Taylor's family and four of his eight children died in infancy, and in 1870 Maria died. Widowed and weakened, Taylor returned to England partly to recuperate but also to develop his new mission. There he married again to a fellow missionary, Jennie Faulding. Taylor's growing role as a missionary speaker bore remarkable fruit and China became a priority for many British believers.

The Work Expands

Taylor was able to return to China with more new workers in 1876, and the next twenty years saw the CIM mission work expand as he and a growing number of co-workers (around a hundred in 1881) planted the gospel ever deeper into China. One extraordinary boost for CIM was the decision of seven talented young men – the 'Cambridge Seven' – to serve in China with the mission.

In foreign tours that now extended to North America, Taylor constantly pleaded for more workers, calling for a thousand missionaries to work in China. He got them but instability in China occurred and in 1900 the 'Boxer Rebellion' broke out in which westerners were brutally targeted. Fifty-eight CIM missionaries and twenty-one children were killed before the rebellion ended. Grieving, but undaunted, Taylor and CIM continued.

Finally, after fifty years in China, Taylor retired to Switzerland with Jennie. Despite having handed over most of his responsibilities, he remained deeply involved with CIM. After Jennie's passing in 1904, he visited China for the eleventh and last time, dying there in 1905.

Taylor's achievements remain truly astonishing. By the end of his life CIM had recruited over 800 missionaries for China and established 200 mission stations with over a hundred thousand Chinese Christians linked with churches. Taylor's influence extended beyond preaching: he instigated medical work, promoted famine relief and encouraged the creation of over a hundred schools. He was also a leader in the campaign against the evils of the opium trade.

Taylor was buried in the city of Zhenjiang, next to his first wife, Maria.

Hudson Taylor is one of the most remarkable figures in Christian history. Spiritually, he had an unquenchable hunger for God. Physically, despite episodes of poor health, he worked tirelessly. He was a gifted preacher, whether in several Chinese languages or English, and a remarkable motivator for missions. He was an outstanding organiser, taking his mission from nothing into one of the largest organisations of its kind.

Three related aspects strike me about Hudson Taylor.

- First, he was someone who was *dependent on God*. Frequently, Taylor found himself in nerve-wracking situations in which he or his mission had desperate needs: in every case, his response was to pray. Although both he and CIM became well acquainted with suffering, he found God faithful and saw remarkable answers to prayer. And although he created a formidable organisation, Taylor never made the mistake of letting it become a substitute for relying on God.

- Second, he was someone who was made ***independent by God***. Taylor's mould-breaking strategies of identifying with a culture, working with women, recruiting ordinary people and crossing denominations transformed missionary work. Although he came under many pressures from governments, authorities and even other missionary organisations, he resisted them. Quite simply, Taylor was someone who took his orders from God alone.

- Finally, he was someone who was ***confident in God***. Faced with evangelising an area almost as big as Europe, Taylor remained undaunted and pressed on. He displayed a boundless confidence that he had been called by God to preach the gospel in China and that the God who had called him could be trusted.

One of Hudson Taylor's quotes summarises his attitude:

'There is a living God.
He has spoken in the Bible.
He means what he says,
and will do all that he has promised.'

AMEN!

Shanghai today. Taylor first arrived here in 1854 and ministered in the city extensively throughout his life.

FRANCIS SCHAEFFER

In my early days as a Christian one of the most influential figures around was the theologian, philosopher, pastor and preacher Francis Schaeffer. I have always valued his books and regret that I didn't spend time with him at L'Abri.

Born in Pennsylvania, USA in 1912, Schaeffer was the only child of working-class parents with no Christian faith.

In his youth he became fascinated by the great questions of philosophy and, finding answers in the Bible, became a Christian at eighteen. After studying in a liberal arts college in Virginia, he enrolled in a theologically conservative seminary to train as a pastor.

In 1935 he married Edith, the daughter of missionaries with Hudson Taylor's China Inland Mission. She was to be an enormous support to Schaeffer and his ministry and together they were to have four children.

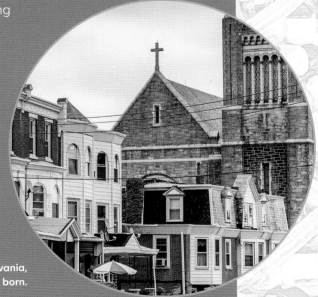

Germantown, Pennsylvania, where Schaeffer was born.

In his early years as a Presbyterian pastor, Schaeffer found himself focusing on defending a Christianity that took the Bible seriously against the increasingly liberal version. After the Second World War, Schaeffer's denomination sent him to investigate the state of Christianity in Europe. He returned with an alarming account of how many European churches were slipping away from any confidence in the Bible as God's word. One lasting influence of the trip came from Schaeffer's many visits to art galleries and museums, something that deepened his lifelong love of western culture.

L'Abri

Soon the Schaeffers felt called by God to be missionaries in Europe and in 1948 moved to Switzerland where they began a ministry that focused on the defence of a biblical Christianity. In 1951 Schaeffer came to the realisation that his calling was to preach truth to those outside Christianity rather than wage theological warfare within it.

Soon the Schaeffers founded a community in the Swiss Alps which they called L'Abri, French for 'the shelter'. Increasingly, young searching people would turn up and stay with the Schaeffers, where Edith would look after them and Francis would listen to them and

Edith and Francis Schaeffer.

Schaeffer at L'Abri
Conference, 1981.

discuss life, philosophy and theology. One of Schaeffer's strengths
was his remarkable breadth of interest and he became known for
how he could apply biblical wisdom to everything from modern art
to contemporary philosophy.

Shelter from the Storm

L'Abri became more well-known and in the 1960s, that decade when
everything was questioned and challenged, it acquired a special
significance. Many who were hungry to find meaning and purpose
or who had been disillusioned by the hippy scene found their way
there. There were conversions but perhaps of equal importance, many
Christians saw broken faith mended and shallow faith deepened as
they stayed with the Schaeffers. For many people L'Abri was indeed
a shelter from the storm.

Increasingly, as Schaeffer's talks were printed and circulated, he
became a global figure and began an important itinerant ministry
which made a remarkable impact. Christian audiences found
themselves faced by a man dressed like a Swiss farmer, with knee
breeches and hiking shoes, a white beard and long hair, confidently
applying biblical Christianity to the confusing world about them.
Whether it was pop music, avant-garde cinema or liberal theology,
Schaeffer always had something helpful and insightful to say. He was
a man who was simultaneously radical, challenging and inspiring.

The Schaeffers founded a community in the Swiss Alps which they called L'Abri, French for 'the shelter'.

In 1978 Schaeffer was diagnosed with cancer, dying from it in 1984.

Cultural Change

Francis Schaeffer left a rich legacy. The work of L'Abri continues in different ways across the world. Most of Schaeffer's books remain in print and many of them are still relevant. Schaeffer could see the big picture. His solemn warning that the West's departure from its Christian foundations would take it into a perilous moral vacuum has sadly been fulfilled. Schaeffer also had a tremendous influence on individuals and many people, including some distinguished academics, view him as their spiritual and intellectual father.

Schaeffer was the right man at the right time, wisely guiding the global church through an upheaval of cultural change. Faced with new and challenging questions many believers were enormously reassured by the fact that, even if they didn't have the answers (or sometimes even understand the questions), Francis Schaeffer did.

As an evangelist, Francis Schaeffer is a hero of mine for various reasons. Let me list three.

- First, Schaeffer **cared about the world**. In difficult times it's always tempting to go into defensive mode and hide behind thick walls. Sadly that hinders evangelism because you don't actually meet anybody there with whom you can share the gospel. With his love of art and culture Schaeffer didn't retreat from the world but sought to apply God's truth to it.

- Second, Schaeffer **cared about truth**. He often spoke of 'true truth'. Yet it holds an important idea; the fact that at a time when there are many claims to 'truth' only Christianity is fundamentally and genuinely true. It's vital in evangelism: we ask people to accept the gospel not because it can make a difference but because it is ultimately true.

- Third, Schaeffer **cared about people**. He could have become a hermit, grappling with ideas in comfort and safety from his Swiss mountain retreat. But he didn't. He and Edith sacrificially opened their house to the world and without judgement cared for those who came to them. Schaeffer softened the sharpness of truth with the sweetness of compassion.

Francis Schaeffer cared about the world, he cared about truth, he cared about people. Do we?

JOHN NEWTON

Few stories in Christian history are more dramatic than that of John Newton, whose life demonstrates the title of his most famous hymn, 'Amazing Grace'.

Newton was born in London in 1725 to a seagoing father and a devout mother. He followed his father to sea at the age of eleven but rejected his mother's faith, becoming a rebellious, reckless and immoral youngster. He had an ability to find trouble: rejecting good jobs, being fired after six sea voyages and, aged nineteen,

This fictitious depiction used by the abolition movement shows a slaver selling a woman into slavery after she saved him from a shipwreck.

Newton's first ventures into the slave trade were in Sierra Leone, West Africa.

Those captured by slave traders were crammed onto slave ships and chained together. Many died before they reached their destination.

press-ganged into the Royal Navy. He deserted, was caught and given a public flogging. Managing to leave the Navy, Newton became involved in the slave trade, shipping slaves from Africa to North America. It's a sad fact that slavery – a profitable and in Britain largely invisible trade – then aroused little controversy. Newton, having made many enemies, found himself left behind in Africa by his colleagues and was there imprisoned in chains and treated brutally for eighteen months.

The Beginnings of Change

When Newton was rescued in 1748 he showed no signs of repentance. Nevertheless, as he sailed back to Britain his ship was struck by a severe storm. As the vessel began to sink Newton began to pray, throwing himself on the mercy of God.

Lough Swilly in County Donegal, the setting of the severe storm.

Somehow the ship was able to make it back safely to the British Isles. Although Newton later considered his prayer to mark the moment of his conversion he was to write,

'I cannot consider myself to have been a believer, in the full sense of the word, until a considerable time afterwards.'

However, change had started and Newton began to pray and to read the Bible.

Olney, Buckinghamshire.

In 1750 Newton married Polly Catlett, with whom he was to have forty years of happy, if childless, marriage. He returned to serve on slave ships, making three voyages as captain and seemingly ignoring any inconsistency between his trade and his faith.

A Growing Faith

At the age of twenty-nine, after ill health, Newton gave up seafaring and instead took a job in the port of Liverpool. There his Christian life started to blossom and he came under the influence of those great preachers of the Methodist revival, John and Charles Wesley and George Whitefield. Newton's life changed and he became involved in evangelical fellowships and in organising Bible study. He sought ordination in the Church of England but for several years was rejected because of his lack of a degree and the suspicion that he had acquired Methodist 'enthusiasm'.

Finally, aided by an influential supporter, Newton was ordained and became curate of Olney in Buckinghamshire. A lively, committed and caring pastor who taught the Bible and preached appealing and relevant sermons, he trebled the size of his congregation. He also wrote books that brought him to the attention of the wider public.

The poet and hymnwriter William Cowper moved to Olney and he and Newton became close friends, something that was to prove an enormous help to the

Hymnwriter William Cowper.

depressive Cowper. Together, they set about writing hymns. Newton's contribution included many hymns that remain popular, including 'Amazing Grace', 'How Sweet the Name of Jesus Sounds' and 'Glorious Things of Thee Are Spoken'. Although technically Cowper may have been the finer poet, Newton demonstrated a remarkable ability for using simple language.

After sixteen years of fruitful ministry in Olney, Newton moved to a City of London church in 1780. There, at the heart of the nation, he was able to be a powerful influencer, encouraging, counselling and promoting in every way, a vibrant evangelical Christianity. When the young and promising politician William Wilberforce became converted and was tempted to leave politics for the church, Newton encouraged him to stay in Parliament and 'serve God where he was'.

Olney Hymns, pg.53. Published in 1779, these verses became known as 'Amazing Grace'.

The End of the Slave Trade

By now the national mood was turning against slavery, and Newton, still grieved over his own involvement decades earlier, wrote a powerful pamphlet – 'Thoughts Upon the African Slave Trade' – based on his own experiences. It circulated widely and was greatly used in helping Wilberforce in his ultimately successful campaign against the slave trade.

In his final years Newton became perhaps the senior statesman of the evangelical church in Britain, doing whatever he could to promote the gospel, supporting ministers across denominations and helping to found both the Church Missionary Society and the Bible Society. Newton died in 1807 aged eighty-two, after fifty years of service to Christ and just months after slavery was ended across the British Empire.

The 2006 movie, *Amazing Grace*, tells the story of the campaign against the slave trade, and highlights Newton's part in that story.

JOHN NEWTON

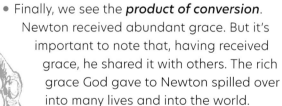

Drawings of *Marie Séraphique*, an 18th-century
slave ship, showing the slave deck

**There are many things to challenge us in John
Newton's life but to me the most striking are
those that arise out of his conversion. Let me
offer you four thoughts.**

- First, we see the *priority of conversion*. The
transformation of Newton from the messiest of
lives to a gracious servant of God teaches the
life-changing potential of an encounter with
Christ. Ultimately, Christianity is not a matter
of morality; it's about Jesus changing lives.

- Second, we see the *principle of conversion*.
Newton's story reminds us that while we cannot
save ourselves, God can and does. In the words
of 'Amazing Grace', Newton came to God as
an undeserving 'wretch' who was 'lost' and
'blind' yet Christ saved him.

- Third, we see the *process of conversion*. We all love stories of
dramatic conversion with overnight changes of behaviour. They
happen but so do seemingly protracted conversions like Newton's.
We need to be reminded that sometimes it may take a long time
after the seed is planted for the flower of faith to blossom.

- Finally, we see the *product of conversion*.
Newton received abundant grace. But it's
important to note that, having received
grace, he shared it with others. The rich
grace God gave to Newton spilled over
into many lives and into the world.

Among John Newton's last recorded
words were these:

*'My memory is nearly gone
but I remember two things:
that I am a great sinner
and Christ is a great saviour.'*

AMEN.

ELISABETH ELLIOT

Elisabeth Elliot was born in 1926 in Brussels to missionary parents who soon relocated to the USA.

There, at an early age, she made a personal profession of faith to follow Christ. Elisabeth soon felt God's call to be a missionary. In 1944, with the intention of becoming a Bible translator, she enrolled at Wheaton College where she met Jim Elliot, who had a similar calling for missions and with whom she had a long romance. After graduation Elisabeth trained as a Bible translator and in 1952 both she and Jim went independently to Ecuador to work as missionaries. Finally, in 1953 she and Jim married in Ecuador where, in 1955, their daughter Valerie was born.

Quito, the capital of Ecuador.

A missionary challenge at the time was a totally unreached Amazonian tribe, then known as the Aucas but now known as the Waodani. Links with this tribe, deep in the rainforest, were almost non-existent and their language was unknown. The Waodani also had a fearsome reputation for violence. (Anthropological studies have revealed that they had the highest rates of homicide ever recorded in a human society.)

Jim Elliot's Murder

Drawn by the challenge of the Waodani, a group of five young American missionary men, including Jim Elliot, decided to try to reach them. After seemingly friendly initial encounters, in January 1956 they flew in only to be suddenly speared to death.

The murder of these five men had an enormous impact in the United States and worldwide. The press focused not just on the events and the 'savage' tribe involved but also on the survivors, notably Elisabeth and baby Valerie. Elisabeth left for the States with her daughter and there, in a matter of weeks, wrote the book *Through Gates of Splendor*. It became a bestseller not simply

A rescue party at the site where Jim Elliot and four others were speared to death.

because of the dramatic events it recounted but because Elisabeth, gifted with both writing ability and deep insight, had produced a remarkably powerful book. In this and subsequent books, Elisabeth's depiction of her husband Jim gave the world a great example of missionary commitment with his inspiring quote:

> *'He is no fool who gives what he cannot keep*
> *to gain that which he cannot lose'.*

Feeling called by God to witness to those who had killed her husband, Elisabeth returned to Ecuador with her daughter. Working amongst an adjacent tribe, she prayed for an opportunity to make contact with the Waodani.

Finally, a Waodani woman appeared, allowing Elisabeth to begin to learn the language and, after being promised safety, Elisabeth, her three-year-old daughter and Rachel Saint (the sister of the murdered pilot) went to live with the Waodani. The world held its breath. The idea that Elisabeth, as a single mother, was taking her little daughter to live with the violent tribe that had killed her husband was stunning. No less shocking in the 1950s was the fact that it was a woman taking the initiative in reaching out to a murderous tribe.

For two years the women and Valerie lived with the Waodani. They were accepted and, learning the language, taught the basics of Christianity. They were able to display forgiveness to those men who had slain the men they had loved, and their living demonstration of what forgiveness meant undermined the fatal Waodani culture of unending family vendettas.

Eventually Elisabeth left the Waodani and worked with another tribe until 1963. Leaving for the States, she then focused on writing and speaking. She taught not just about missions work but also about many aspects of Christian living. As the 1960s brought enormous cultural changes, she found herself commenting on the role of women, where this most courageous of women took a position against feminism.

In 1969 Elisabeth married again, to a professor of theology. Tragically, he died from cancer in 1973. A widow once more, Elisabeth continued her worldwide ministry, marrying for a third time in 1977 to a hospital chaplain. For thirteen years she hosted a daily Christian radio programme. With the new century it soon became apparent that Elisabeth was beginning to suffer from dementia and she gave up public speaking before dying in 2015.

Let me highlight three things that are striking in Elisabeth Elliot's long life of faith.

- First, her faith showed a deep *obedience* to God. Elisabeth saw Christianity as something that involved a discipleship of complete obedience to Christ. It was such a discipleship that compelled her

Elliot died in Magnolia, Massachussetts in 2015.

to meet with her husband's killers and forgive them. When asked to justify missionary work she simply pointed out that the church remained under the orders given by Christ. Elisabeth was convinced: to belong to Christ was to obey him.

• Second, her faith was marked by a profound *acceptance* of God. Elisabeth grappled with the suffering she experienced; the death of two husbands, the murder of fellow workers and many other struggles. She rejected any attempt to find explanations for such events. Importantly, she taught that we must accept what we are given from God precisely because he is God. The path of obedience often leads through deep water: explanations can wait till heaven.

Ruth Graham, wife of Billy Graham, reads Elliot's book *Through Gates of Splendor*.

• Finally, Elisabeth's faith gave her a sturdy *independence* before the world. All Christian communication can either be comforting or challenging and what Elisabeth said and wrote was always the latter. Quite simply, she refused to give what people demanded. After Elisabeth went to the Waodani there was an expectation that she would confirm the view that they were appalling savages. Instead, she wrote compellingly of how the people she had come to love had both vices and virtues. Her concern to say what she felt God wanted her to say made her independent of all other pressures.

The faithful and fruitful life of Elisabeth Elliot sets a challenging example of discipleship to us today. She deserves to be remembered.

WILLIAM BOOTH

William Booth was born in Nottingham in 1829 into a family where wealth, education and religion were in short supply.

In his early teens he started work and at the age of fifteen came to faith in Christ in a Methodist chapel. He wrote in his diary: 'God shall have all there is of William Booth.' Shortly afterwards he encountered open public evangelistic meetings with lively songs, a powerful message and an 'altar call'. Sensing this was where his calling lay, Booth began open-air evangelism, particularly amongst the poor.

There was no shortage of opportunity. The Industrial Revolution had sent vast numbers of people into the towns seeking work and the result was crowded, unsanitary and impoverished slums, full of social problems. With few exceptions, the established churches, formal and middle-class, were unwilling to be involved.

Booth became a Methodist minister but felt drawn to a purely evangelistic ministry. He met Catherine Mumford and they were married in 1855. It was to be the most supportive and productive of marriages: they had eight children, most of whom became leaders in the Salvation Army.

Booth was born in Sneinton, Nottingham.

Booth soon resigned his pastorate and, as itinerant preachers, he and Catherine travelled across England and Wales. In 1865 the Booths settled in east London amidst appalling social problems. Here he started a Christian mission work which sought not only to save souls but also to feed bodies. He wrote:

'You cannot warm the hearts of people with God's love if they have an empty stomach and cold feet.'

'The Christian Mission' as set out by Booth.

The Salvation Army

In 1878 Booth formalised his mission organisation into what he termed the 'Salvation Army'. The military theme was seen not just in the uniforms and ranks but also in a disciplined structure. 'General Booth', as he was now known, gave the Army its motto 'Blood and Fire', referring to the blood of Christ and the purifying power of the Holy Spirit, and it summed up the new organisation's forceful and determined mood.

The Army rapidly won converts. Their meetings were accessible to those who would never dare to attend a conventional church. Here they received food for their bodies, sang songs to lively tunes and heard converts giving their testimonies and preachers using ordinary language. Above all, there was acceptance: any judgement was to do with sin, not social status. Joining the Army was also appealing because with the uniform came purpose, identity and a sense of belonging.

Booth's first motor tour was in 1904. Many tours followed until he was 'promoted to glory' in 1912.

WILLIAM BOOTH

The Salvation Army emblem.

The Salvationists faced much opposition. Many churches criticised the new movement for the way that they worked with the poor. More aggressive opposition came from those who were offended by the Army's rejection of alcohol and its determined and very visible presence in even the worst areas. The Salvationists, who put up no resistance, made an easy target for their opponents and there were injuries and deaths. Yet the opposition simply united the Army and gave it publicity. Soon Salvation Army units were being formed across Europe, the United States and Australia.

A Global Legacy

Increasingly, the Salvation Army became an important force in providing social relief. In 1890 Booth published *In Darkest England and the Way Out*, a book that not only identified the nation's ills but proposed ambitious projects to help the poor, ex-prisoners and the homeless. Widely read and very influential, many of its pioneering ideas were developed in the twentieth century. One paragraph that struck me when I read his book was:

I consider that the chief dangers which confront the coming century will be religion without the Holy Ghost, Christianity without Christ, forgiveness without repentance, salvation without regeneration, politics without God, and heaven without hell.

These words couldn't be more relevant today.

After thirty-five years of marriage, Catherine Booth died in 1890. William Booth pressed on as the honoured leader of what was now a global ministry. In the last decade of his life he travelled worldwide, meeting kings, emperors

Catherine Booth.

Mount William Booth was named in 1965. It is part of the Ram Range in Alberta, Canada.

and presidents. His death in 1912 was greeted by scenes of extraordinary national mourning. His finest memorial is, of course, the Salvation Army that he founded, which today has 1.7 million members in 119 countries.

Let me suggest four striking elements in William Booth's achievement.

- First, I find a remarkable *innovation*. Many people had been doing work with the poor in various ways, but Booth's genius was somehow to bring together the ingredients of help, evangelism, support and discipleship to produce a formula that, in the Salvation Army, was so spectacularly successful.

- Second, I am struck by his astonishing *intuition*. Booth was a man who made his decisions not so much by analysis as by sheer God-given instinct. Looking back, with all our knowledge of organisational structure and mission, Booth got so much right. Through his pattern of uniforms, music, songs and discipline he built an organisation that those in need wanted to belong to.

WILLIAM BOOTH

• Third, I am struck by the way his ministry was **integrated**. Booth believed that people needed to hear the good news of Jesus Christ but that preaching to them when they were hungry was pointless. These days we would call this 'holistic mission' and praise it; Booth pioneered it.

• Finally, I'm struck by how Booth's ministry was marked by **independence**. He never waited for consensus or collaboration and cared little for what other people or other denominations thought. When he couldn't find a supportive denomination, he created his own. Although this stubborn independence – so often a necessity with pioneers – allowed him to achieve so much so fast.

William Booth wrote:

While women weep, as they do now, I'll fight; while little children go hungry, as they do now, I'll fight; while men go to prison, in and out, in and out, as they do now, I'll fight; while there is a drunkard left, while there is a poor lost girl upon the streets, while there remains one dark soul without the light of God, I'll fight, I'll fight to the very end!

At his conversion Booth promised God everything that there was of him. I think he kept that promise and I think that God richly honoured it. May we, too, promise God everything that there is of us.

In Darkest England and the Way Out, Salvation Army Social Campaign (1890).

HARRIET
BEECHER
STOWE

In the nineteenth century Harriet Beecher Stowe was the most important woman in the United States. It is reported that during the American Civil War, when she was introduced to President Lincoln he said, 'So this is the little woman who gave us this great war.'

Harriet was born in Connecticut into the Beecher family, a distinguished American dynasty. Her father was a famed Christian preacher and Harriet grew up in a godly family that promoted progressive social causes, such as the abolition of slavery and the education of women. Harriet, intelligent and well educated, underwent a conversion experience in her teens that was to affect who she was for the rest of her life.

When Harriet was twenty-one the family moved to Cincinnati, Ohio, where she became a teacher. Although Ohio banned the holding of slaves, it bordered Kentucky where slavery was legal,

Stowe was born in Litchfield, Connecticut (USA).

The house in Brunswick, Maine (USA) where Stowe wrote *Uncle Tom's Cabin*.

and in Cincinnati Harriet encountered many escaped slaves. Harriet's objections to slavery deepened when visiting Kentucky she saw families being broken up and sold at slave auctions. Her loathing of slavery was supported by her faith: after all, if a slave was a child of God, what right did anyone have to buy or sell them?

Harriet became friends with Calvin Stowe, a professor of theology. After his wife died, Calvin married Harriet in 1836 and they had a long marriage with seven children. Moving back with her husband to New England, the Stowes were involved in the Underground Railway, the network of individuals that helped slaves flee to safety. As they housed fugitives, Harriet listened to their sad stories.

Uncle Tom's Cabin

In 1851 she was asked to write for an abolitionist newspaper. Following the pattern established by authors like Dickens, she started a novel in weekly instalments. It was a great success, running to forty instalments, and was published as a book. *Uncle Tom's Cabin*, as it was titled, is an involving novel that deals openly with the horrors of slavery.

An early edition of *Uncle Tom's Cabin*.

It ends with Uncle Tom, a noble and humble Christian slave, being beaten to death by his master because he refuses to reveal the location of two escapees. With his final words, Tom offers forgiveness and utters an appeal for conversion.

The passionate and emotional storyline of *Uncle Tom's Cabin* had an extraordinary impact on people and appealed powerfully against slavery. The first blockbuster novel, it broke publishing records, selling a million copies in the States before the Civil War. It was a global success with well over a million copies sold in Britain alone.

Changing the Course of History

Understandably, many African-Americans were troubled by the way that Uncle Tom lets himself be beaten to death by a white man. Yet the book did have an astonishing impact. Did it cause the American Civil War? Probably not, but it did make slavery morally indefensible and may have helped the abolitionist Abraham Lincoln become president. Nevertheless, it did play its part in the war. Britain, with its enormous cotton industry, was tempted to support the South – an action that would probably have changed the course of the war – but the enormous success of Harriet's book made that politically unacceptable.

President Abraham Lincoln.

Harriet continued to write books and undertook national and international tours. She made three trips to Europe where she met with crowds and with Charles Dickens and Queen Victoria. She remained committed to social reform in such areas as better legal rights for women and opportunities for education for the newly liberated slaves. She and her husband continued to live modestly and she donated much of her considerable profits to good causes. Following the death of her husband, Harriet's mental health declined and she died in 1895.

HARRIET BEECHER STOWE

What can we learn from Harriet Beecher Stowe? Thinking about the remarkable achievement that is *Uncle Tom's Cabin*, I note four intriguing and challenging elements.

- First, Harriet was a woman who was *ready*. It's been said that 'fortune favours the prepared mind'. A similar but overlooked phenomenon occurs in the Christian life: prepared people find that God gives them things to do. Harriet, deep-rooted in the Christian faith, Bible knowledge and committed to social action, was certainly prepared. All that was needed was the trigger of that request to write against slavery. Are we making it a priority to prepare ourselves for God to use us?

- Second, Harriet *reacted*. One of the troubling features of slavery is how so many people conveniently managed to overlook it as a moral issue. Harriet not only saw what slavery entailed but her offended conscience demanded that she took action. We live at a time when there are plenty of overlooked outrages and we need more Christians with Harriet's enthusiasm to notice them and react wisely.

- Third, Harriet *responded*. Her gift was storytelling and that's what she did. The horror of slavery might seem to have demanded more, but what she was able to do turned out to be remarkably effective. What gifts do we have that can be used to make a difference? Let's use them!

- Finally, I see how God brought *results*. As with the boy with the five barley loaves and two small fish in John's account of the feeding of the five thousand, God delights in making much out of little. God achieved much through Harriet Beecher Stowe. He can use us too.

Slave auction scene in *Uncle Tom's Cabin*.

DIETRICH BONHOEFFER

Dietrich Bonhoeffer, executed for his long-standing opposition to Hitler, is one of the great Christian heroes of the twentieth century.

Bonhoeffer was born in 1906 to an aristocratic German family. Evidently gifted, he chose to study theology, graduating with a doctorate at the age of twenty-one. In the first of what were to be many international links he worked for two years with a German congregation in Barcelona. He then went to the United States to study for a year at a liberal theological college that he found shallow and uninspiring. He was, however, impressed by the African-American churches he worshipped at, appreciating the congregations' zeal and sympathising with the social injustices they endured.

Bonhoeffer returned to Germany in 1931, lecturing and pastoring a church. Horrified by the rise of the Nazis he spoke out publicly against Hitler from the moment he became Chancellor in 1933. His was not a popular view: many German Christians, encouraged by Hitler's manipulative use of Christian language, saw him as the nation's saviour.

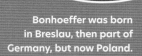

Bonhoeffer was born in Breslau, then part of Germany, but now Poland.

DIETRICH BONHOEFFER

Synodal elections in 1933: German Christians and Confessing Church campaigners in Berlin.

Bonhoeffer found himself part of the resistance against Nazism. He spoke against the persecution of the Jews and when Hitler demanded a church that swore loyalty to him, Bonhoeffer helped create the Confessing Church which declared that its head was Christ not the Führer. Bonhoeffer gained only limited support and, disillusioned, he went to pastor two German-speaking churches in London. There, watching with alarm the direction Germany was taking, he made important friendships with British church leaders.

Cheap Grace

Returning to Germany, Bonhoeffer was soon denounced as a pacifist and an enemy of the state. In 1937 he became involved in the secret training of pastors for the Confessing Church. He also wrote one of his most important books, *The Cost of Discipleship*, in which he rebuked shallow Christianity that he termed cheap grace:

'The preaching of forgiveness
without requiring repentance,
baptism without church discipline,
communion without confession . . .
Cheap grace is grace without discipleship,
grace without the cross,
grace without Jesus Christ,
living and incarnate.'

It is a warning that continues to be valid today.

Left: Monument to Bonhoeffer, Church of St Peter, Hamburg (Germany).

With war looming, Bonhoeffer, committed to peace and refusing to swear allegiance to Hitler, realised that he could be executed. An opportunity to escape conscription appeared with an invitation to teach in the USA. Bonhoeffer left in June 1939, yet once in the States he realised that he could not be absent from his own country at a time of war and within two weeks took the boat back to Germany.

The Lesser of Evils

When war did break out, Bonhoeffer found himself drawn into the circle of those patriotic Germans who sought to overthrow Hitler. In order to escape conscription he joined the German military intelligence agency, a body which included many who were opposed to Hitler. On paper his task was to use his many international church links to advise the military, but in reality he used them to try to find support for the German resistance.

As the war went on Bonhoeffer found himself on the edges of various plots to assassinate Hitler. Increasingly aware of the horrors the Third Reich was unleashing, he found himself reluctantly concluding that the assassination of Hitler would be the lesser of evils.

In 1943 Bonhoeffer became engaged to Maria von Wedemeyer but shortly afterwards his role in helping Jews escape to Switzerland was uncovered by the Gestapo and he was arrested. At first he was able to write and receive visitors who supplied him with books and took away

Bonhoeffer plays piano with his young nephew and godson, Christoph von Dohnányi, who went on to be a famous German conductor.

DIETRICH BONHOEFFER

his writings; many of these were incorporated into another classic book, *Letters and Papers from Prison*.

In July 1944 Bonhoeffer's imprisonment became more severe and he was sent to Buchenwald concentration camp. The accounts we have of him at this time describe him as a man of peace, full of grace and kindness, and occupied in pastoring and counselling those about him.

Execution

In the spring of 1945 Bonhoeffer's name was linked with an old plot against Hitler and his execution ordered. He was hanged on 9th April 1945, just two weeks before the camp was liberated. His last recorded words were,

'This is the end – for me the beginning of life.'

National GDR Monument, Buchenwald concentration camp.

I find at least four striking things in the faith of Dietrich Bonhoeffer.

- First, his faith was displayed in *doing*. Bonhoeffer could have stayed an academic theologian quietly writing. Instead, he insisted that Christianity had to be lived out and to be a disciple of Christ was to *do* something. Beliefs must have consequences: whether it was to work for good or against evil. Bonhoeffer was no armchair Christian and we shouldn't be either.

Statues to modern martyrs above the Great West Door of Westminster Abbey.

- Second, his faith was displayed in *daring*. One of the first German Christians to denounce Hitler, Bonhoeffer worked against Nazism for twelve years, knowing that at any moment he could be - as ultimately he was - arrested, imprisoned and killed. It's particularly hard not to be impressed by how, having made the safety of New York in 1939, Bonhoeffer then took the boat back to Germany. We could do with a lot more daring today.

- Third, his faith was displayed in *defying*. Faced with a threatening government and a church that remained silent, Bonhoeffer spoke out boldly against both. There are times when we, too, need to stand up and speak boldly.

- Finally, and it's uncomfortable, Bonhoeffer's faith was displayed in *dying*. As he wrote in *The Cost of Discipleship*, 'When Christ calls a man, he bids him come and die.' And with typical consistency that is exactly what Bonhoeffer did.

High above Westminster Abbey's West Door are statues of ten modern martyrs and there stands the figure of Dietrich Bonhoeffer. He deserves that place.

FANNY CROSBY

Fanny Crosby was a prolific hymnist, writing more than 8,000 hymns and gospel songs, and the most remarkable thing about her was that she did so in spite of her blindness.

Born in 1820 north of New York, Fanny lost her sight to an eye infection and medical ignorance at the age of six weeks.

Her blindness means that all the existing photographs show her with dark glasses and give the impression of a solemn, formal and very stern woman. The reality was very different: Fanny was an exuberant, warm and cheerful individual.

To be sightless in an age with little concern for the blind, without guide dogs and Braille books, was difficult. Nevertheless, Fanny was raised in a family determined to give her the best possible education and was read Bible passages. Fanny made an early commitment to follow Christ and developed a remarkable memory, learning whole books of the Bible by heart.

Fanny's formal education did not begin until when, aged fifteen, she went to the New York Institute for the Blind, a pioneering institution

Crosby's birthplace.

Crosby was born in the village of Brewster, about 50 miles north of New York City.

where she was to spend twenty-three years: twelve as a student and eleven as a teacher. She developed her singing and learned to play a variety of instruments. The Institute also encouraged her to progress with her gift of composing poetry. An able speaker, Fanny campaigned for better education of the blind and, as part of this, became the first woman to speak in the United States Senate.

An Extraordinary Lyricist

Fanny had always expressed her faith in poems and songs and she increasingly became sought after as a writer of Christian lyrics. Despite a growing reputation as a conference speaker and preacher, she remained deeply involved with her church. Ignoring her blindness and the fact she was under five-foot tall, Fanny became involved in Christian social work amongst the poor of New York and even acted as a nurse during the devastating 1849 cholera epidemic.

Crosby lived in New York for many decades, in areas such as Hell's Kitchen.

In 1858 Fanny married Alexander van Alstyne, a blind church organist. They had one daughter who died shortly after birth: an event that may have prompted Fanny's famous hymn 'Safe in the Arms of Jesus'. Fanny lived on to 1915, dying at the then remarkable age of ninety-four.

FANNY CROSBY

Crosby with van Alstyne.

Fanny had an astonishing ability to write lyrics; she would compose them in her mind and then dictate them to be written down. She could work at incredible speed, sometimes creating seven songs a day. For thirty years she wrote songs for Ira Sankey, the singer who accompanied the evangelist D.L. Moody on his remarkable evangelistic campaigns, and many people made decisions for Christ as her words were sung. Many of Fanny's hymns are still sung in church today. They include 'Blessed Assurance', 'All the Way My Saviour Leads Me', 'Praise Him, Praise Him', 'To God Be the Glory' and 'Jesus Keep Me Near the Cross'.

Revolutionising Christian Music

Fanny wrote warm and memorable verses that appealed to both the mind and the heart. Consider just a few of her best-known lines:

> 'All the way my Saviour leads me;
> What have I to ask beside?
> Can I doubt his tender mercy,
> Who through life has been my guide?'

> 'Blessed assurance, Jesus is mine;
> Oh, what a foretaste of glory divine!
> Heir of salvation, purchase of God,
> Born of his Spirit, washed in his blood.
> This is my story, this is my song,
> Praising my Saviour all the day long.'

Fanny's theology was simple and Christ-centred. Significantly, in an America that was increasingly receiving immigrants with poor English, her words were both easy to understand and to translate. Her accessible songs revolutionised Christian music, opening the way to simpler, gentler songs and so, ultimately, to 'gospel music' and modern worship songs. In 1975 she was posthumously inducted into the Gospel Music Hall of Fame.

Fanny Crosby's Life-Story (1903).

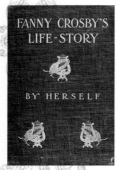

Fanny Crosby was a truly extraordinary woman and I find three challenges in her life.

In 1911, Crosby spoke to 5,000 people at Carnegie Hall, New York.

• First, she displayed a remarkable **commitment** to the gospel. Let's face it, no one writes 8,000 songs without a very serious level of dedication! In her songs Fanny spoke not only of her own faith but also of her burning desire for others to come to Jesus. She claimed she wanted to introduce a million people to Christ through her songs: she may well have exceeded that number! Fanny showed her commitment not just in her words but in her social work. She did indeed give Jesus everything.

• Second, she achieved a remarkable **communication** of the gospel. Evangelism is about communicating clearly, concisely and compassionately the good news of Jesus Christ, and in this Fanny Crosby was a remarkable communicator and evangelist.

• Finally, she displayed a delightful **contentment** in the gospel. In a life of disability, difficulties and disappointments, Fanny didn't just find comfort in Jesus Christ, she found contentment. Her first verse, written at age eight, echoed her lifelong refusal to feel sorry for herself:

'Tis Evening Brings My Heart to Thee' words by Miss Fanny Crosby, 1856.

Oh! what a happy soul I am!
Although I cannot see,
I am resolved that in this world
Contented I will be.

May we too live contented lives and exude joy in Christ despite disappointments and restrictions.

FRANCIS OF ASSISI

Francis of Assisi is apparently the world's most popular saint, but much of this popularity is for the 'legendary Francis'; an amiable, uncontroversial spiritual figure who loved animals, proclaimed peace and endorsed the simple lifestyle. Behind this largely imaginary individual lies the real Francis, a man who is not just authentic but also much more challenging.

Francis was born in the Italian town of Assisi in 1181 to a prosperous family and grew up to become a young man who lived for pleasure. Slowly, after imprisonment during a local war and having had a vision of God, a conversion process began. Francis publicly repented of his life and attitudes, and as he wandered alone through the countryside, Francis had a second vision in which Christ told him to 'repair my house'.

Taking a vow of poverty, Francis began preaching, restoring church buildings and caring for lepers. Francis soon began to attract followers. He imposed simple but strict commands on them: to follow Jesus' teaching, to wear simple clothing, to preach repentance, love and peace, and to perform acts of kindness. In creating his religious community, Francis - who was never ever a

Francis' birthplace.

192

priest – was operating without the authority of the church, a risky process at a time where heresies were brutally treated. In 1209 he went to Rome to see the Pope who reluctantly gave him authorisation.

Back in Assisi, Francis created rules for what became known as the Franciscan Order. Soon he had to form two other orders: one for women and another for those who could not join him full-time. Although a man of great prayer, Francis had evangelistic zeal, preached regularly in streets and markets, and sent his followers out as evangelists across Europe. Feeling personally called to witness to Muslims, Francis made several attempts to reach the Arab world.

Modern-day markets in northern Italy.

Sailing to Egypt

Finally, in 1219 he sailed to Egypt in the middle of the Fifth Crusade with the goal of seeing the Sultan of Egypt converted. Crossing over to the Muslim lines during a ceasefire, he was captured and brought before the Sultan to whom he spoke about Jesus for several days.

Although the Sultan was never (at least openly) a convert, he was impressed enough to allow Francis safe passage back to Italy, where he was forced to be a manager in order to mobilise his multiplying followers into organisational structures that would outlast him.

Modern-day Alexandria.

Basilica of St Francis in Assisia, Umbria (Italy).

That done, Francis, who disliked management, handed over leadership of the three orders. Having struggled with poor health since his visit to Egypt, Francis now became seriously ill. He died in 1226 at the age of only forty-four. Within a few years Francis was canonised as a saint by the Catholic Church, a title that, with his humility and simplicity, he would have no doubt rejected.

In thinking about Francis, let me mention what he *didn't* do. The authentic Francis never said, 'Preach the gospel at all times and use words if necessary.' In fact, as an evangelist who proclaimed the gospel everywhere to everyone, Francis would have strongly rejected the phrase. As do I. Neither did he write the so-called 'Prayer of St Francis' ('Lord, make me an instrument of your peace. Where there is hatred, let me bring love . . .'). That's probably twentieth-century and also talks too much about 'I' and 'me' and too little about Jesus to be authentic. Finally, Francis probably didn't persuade a wolf to stop eating people and he almost certainly didn't preach to the birds, although he loved them.

The Handiwork of God

What's truly important about Francis is what he *did* do. With its simplicity and enthusiasm his ministry was a wake-up call to the church, and the three Franciscan orders he founded have continued to the present day. The authentic Francis did love the natural world but we need to note that he cherished nature because he saw God's handiwork in it. Although not a prolific writer – he was too busy praying and preaching – Francis left some fascinating instructions, prayers and poems. One of these,

which has given us the hymn 'All Creatures of Our God and King', is the *Canticle of the Sun* in which Francis thanks God for the sun, moon, wind, water, fire, earth and even death who are his 'brothers and sisters' and through whom God is praised.

The real problem with the 'legendary Francis' is that it allows the creation of a universal figure that suits everyone, whatever their beliefs, and softens the impact of a remarkable and challenging man. The real Francis raises questions for all Christians.

Franciscans, walking in ancient Assisi.

- First, how seriously are we **committed to our spiritual life**? Francis sought to walk as close to God as he could, seeking a holy simplicity of life in order that nothing would get in the way of encountering and knowing God. Here, Francis is a reminder of the simple but vital truth that Christians must put God first.

- Second, how seriously are we **committed to those who are suffering**? Francis made the care of the poor and downtrodden a priority in his ministry. I think that is a correct and biblical emphasis. Yet supporting the needy is costly in every way and it's easy to let it slide into the margins of our faith. Here, Francis reminds us that if our faith is to be genuine, we must not neglect those who are struggling in whatever way.

- Third, how seriously are we **committed to sharing the good news**? Francis was a man who risked everything to share Jesus with those who seemed to be Christianity's bitterest enemies. Here he is a reminder that it is our duty and our privilege to share the gospel.

Francis challenged the church and Christians of his time; he continues to do so today.

MILDRED CABLE

One truly notable Christian woman is Mildred Cable: missionary to China, a pioneering explorer and writer.

Born in Guildford in 1878 to a family with a deep Christian faith, Mildred accepted Christ at the age of twelve and soon felt God's call to mission. One of the first women students at London University, she learnt medical skills suitable for the mission field. She sensed a calling to China and became engaged to a man who shared her vision. In 1900 the Boxer Rebellion occurred with the murders of many missionaries and their children in China, and her fiancé decided that China was not for him. He gave Mildred a choice: stay in Britain with him or go on her own. She went to China.

Arriving in 1901, she was sent by Hudson Taylor's China Inland Mission (CIM) to northern China to work under the supervision of Eva French (another missionary), and in 1910, Eva's younger sister Francesca joined them; together they formed a remarkable trio whose close friendship lasted for half a century.

Mildred and the sisters learnt Chinese, adopted local dress and identified with the local culture. Although involved in preaching and church leading, their main work lay with a girls' school. Anxious to remedy the

Cable was born in Guildford, Surrey (England).

way that women had been marginalised, they taught the girls not only Christianity but also literacy, science and the Chinese classics. The school and its impact grew rapidly.

Believing that the church and educational system must be ultimately run by the Chinese themselves, the trio worked at developing local leadership. By the early 1920s they felt that this had been achieved to the point where they should look elsewhere for further ministry. Aware that the vast area of western China remained largely unreached by missionaries, they proposed to the CIM that they travel along the ancient Silk Road deep into Central Asia to evangelise. With reluctance, the leadership of the CIM gave them permission.

Eva French, Francesca French, Mildred Cable (L-R).

Beyond the Great Wall

In 1923, taking a mule-drawn cart filled with Christian literature and accompanied by a few local supporters, the trio went beyond the Great Wall. It was the start of fifteen years of remarkable travels in which the trio made five trips, each lasting months. The region was a challenge: frequently waterless, freezing in winter and baking in summer. It was also dangerously unstable, with many different tribes, often ruled by bandits and militias. As they travelled westwards the control of China waned and they had to learn other languages.

Great Wall of China.

Cable travelled extensively in the mountinous regions between Mongolia and China.

The few previous Europeans in the area had been men travelling in well-protected convoys who chose to have only limited contact with the local population. In contrast, the women travelled light and lived amongst the local people, often staying overnight in primitive local inns where they would preach around the campfires.

Reaching New Frontiers

When the trio reached a settlement they would preach in marketplaces where, as western women, they drew large curious crowds to whom they gave away Bibles and Scripture portions. They became acquainted with local warlords and governors, with whom they shared the good news of Jesus. Moving increasingly into Muslim territory they developed a particular ministry amongst women. Eventually their travels took them to China's frontiers with India, Tibet and Russia, and over much of the area they travelled they were probably the first Christian missionaries since the sixth century.

The trio journeyed as far as Tibet.

Missionaries and Explorers

In 1936, with worsening instability, the trio left China for the final time. In Britain they became speakers, with Mildred lecturing to the Royal Geographical Society and all three women meeting royalty. Their fame was helped by nearly twenty books written by Mildred with Eva French's help. Mildred was an observant and sympathetic writer and her books became enormously popular, with some still considered classics of travel literature. None of the trio ever really retired and all gave themselves to ministry. After the Second World War Mildred travelled globally, speaking about Christian mission. She died in 1952 at the age of seventy-four, with Eva and Francesca dying in 1960.

Left: Rainbow Mountains in Zhangye National Geopark, Gansu (China).

Although much of the trio's fame centres on their extraordinary travels they were never just explorers but always those concerned to preach to all about Jesus. Their vision extended beyond spiritual matters: they gave medical aid and encouraged literacy, particularly amongst women. Sometimes their concern was very practical: Mildred was to adopt an abused seven-year-old deaf-mute girl she encountered.

I'm struck by much in the life of Mildred Cable but let me mention three things.

- First, her *sacrifice*. Heroically, Mildred gave up marriage for the sake of the gospel. Significantly, however, she did not become a solitary individual but developed the closest of friendships with two other women. Nothing about her life suggests any sense of loneliness, regret or frustration.

- Second, her *sensitivity*. It is often alleged that missionaries are insensitive to local cultures but that cannot be said of Mildred. Her writings reveal both an affection for China and its people and a deep and scholarly respect for its culture.

- Finally, her *strategy*. Mildred worked at educating women not just to emancipate them but because she believed they could spread the gospel. She took the Silk Road because she knew that along it she would be able to share Jesus with travellers from unreached countries. She trained and taught people so that they could, in turn, do the same for others. Behind Mildred's strategy, I sense God's. Unknown to all, the century-old open door for missions in China was closing. The trio's evangelistic trips into the wilds of Central Asia allowed them to seize an opportunity that was soon to end.

The region they worked in may largely be closed for open mission work today, but this troubled world has many other hard places that need the sort of adventurous and faithful witness that Mildred Cable displayed.

MARTYN LLOYD-JONES

Martyn Lloyd-Jones was born in Wales in 1899 and lived there until he was a teenager when his family moved to London.

Despite spending most of his life in London, Lloyd-Jones never lost either his Welsh language or his Welsh identity. He studied medicine and began to rise rapidly in the medical profession. His life changed when he had a series of deep experiences of God which gave him a love and zeal for Christ. Soon, despite having the most promising of medical careers before him, Lloyd-Jones felt called to preach. In 1927, without any formal theological training, he left medicine and, taking a massive salary cut, went with his wife Bethan to pastor a struggling church in Port Talbot, one of the poorest areas of South Wales.

Port Talbot (Wales).

'If we only spent more of our time in looking at him, we should soon forget ourselves.'

MARTYN LLOYD-JONES

There, Lloyd-Jones's church grew rapidly and saw remarkable conversions. The reputation of 'the Doctor', as he was increasingly referred to, became widespread. In 1939 Lloyd-Jones returned to London to become associate pastor at Westminster Chapel, one of the capital's largest nonconformist churches, becoming its pastor in 1943. For the next twenty-five years, as the world changed about him, the Doctor preached faithfully and consistently filled the 1,500-seater Westminster Chapel. Lloyd-Jones was involved in many things: conference speaking, training of preachers and ministry amongst students. But it was his regular weekly preaching – once on Friday evening, twice on Sunday – where his impact was most felt.

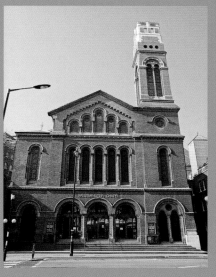

Westminster Chapel.

An Iconic Preacher

The Doctor's preaching ministry was a phenomenon and the painstaking way in which he dealt with Bible books became legendary. So for example, he preached on Romans for twelve years on Friday nights with 366 sermons published in fourteen volumes. Most of his sermons are still in print and many of the later ones were recorded. Lloyd-Jones's preaching was always serious, clear and logical. What his sermons had was a sense of the presence of God. In 1968 ill-health finally forced the Doctor's retirement, but he continued writing and teaching until his death in 1981.

Lloyd-Jones's Influences

There were three great influences on Lloyd-Jones. The first was his Welsh identity and his awareness of a nation periodically transformed by great revivals given by God. The second was his love of the seventeenth-century Puritans; he himself was often described as the 'last of the Puritan preachers'. The third was his

MARTYN LLOYD-JONES

Lloyd-Jones never lost his strong Welsh identity.

medical training, which gave him his analytical approach and his calm, precise diagnostic preaching in which he sought to identify both problems and cures.

As an evangelist, what encourages me is Lloyd-Jones's supreme commitment to preaching. He saw his life's work as publicly declaring the gospel so that men and women would be converted to Christ and built up in the faith. Beneath his calm, measured language in the pulpit was a profound passion to see people born-again and strengthened as believers. An enduring legacy from this is his wonderful book, *Preaching and Preachers*, which I have found to be extraordinarily helpful.

Here are some of my favourite Martyn Lloyd-Jones quotations:

'You are either a Christian or you are not a Christian; you cannot be partly a Christian. You are either "dead" or "alive"; you are either "born" or "not born".'

'Have you realised that most of your unhappiness in life is due to the fact that you are listening to yourself instead of talking to yourself.'

'The church is always to be under the Word: she must be; we must keep her there. You must not assume that because the church started correctly, she will continue so. She did not do so in the New Testament times; she has not done so since. Without being constantly reformed by the Word, the church becomes something very different.'

Let me suggest three things about Lloyd-Jones's preaching that are challenging.

• First, his preaching was ***biblical***. The Doctor had an unshakeable trust in Scripture as the written word of God. Although never formally trained in theology, Lloyd-Jones was well read and was all too aware of how the liberal theology which watered-down the Bible was infecting churches. Lloyd-Jones rejected liberalism and instead preached with confidence in the truth and relevance

Newcastle Emlyn, where Lloyd-Jones was buried.

of God's word. This high view of Scripture could also be seen in the way that in preaching, his goal was always to simply let God speak. I believe the Doctor was right and indeed that history has vindicated him. Liberalism has produced no fruit.

- Second, his preaching was *spiritual*. Lloyd-Jones may have been the 'last of the Puritans' and had a deep commitment to Reformed theology but he never fell into the temptation to simply proclaim some correct and formal faith. He was a man who preached with a firm expectation that the Holy Spirit would work. Indeed, the Doctor encouraged Christians to seek the deepest possible experience of the Spirit in their lives. Longing for revival, he prayed for God's Spirit to move in power, in people and in nations. So should we.

- Third, his preaching was *pastoral*. In a way, Lloyd-Jones never outgrew his medical training; he simply switched to caring for souls. In his sermons we often hear him speak of diagnosis and prescription; he saw humanity as deeply diseased by sin and in desperate need of God's healing through Christ. One lasting testimony to this approach is another excellent book, *Spiritual Depression: Its Causes and Its Cure*, a volume that has helped many who have found themselves struggling in life.

Like all of us, Lloyd-Jones was a man of his time, but what he proclaimed was eternally true. That's the challenge for us all!

HANNAH MORE

Hannah More was born in 1745 near Bristol, the fourth of five daughters of a schoolmaster.

At a time when only upper-class women had a formal education, her father ensured she and her sisters were well taught. She studied at her father's school for girls and, while still a teenager, taught there. Hannah wrote her first play for her pupils and became involved with the theatrical world of Bristol.

At the age of twenty-two Hannah became engaged to a wealthy landowner who kept postponing their wedding. When after six years the engagement was broken off, he gave Hannah, as compensation, an annual allowance that allowed her to devote herself to writing. Hannah never married.

Experiencing Christ

Hannah's poetry was published to acclaim and her plays were successfully staged not just in Britain but in other countries. She began visiting London where, as an intelligent conversationalist, she rapidly became part of the world of actors, painters and thinkers, as well as the gathering of female intellectuals known as the 'Bluestocking circle'.

Fishponds, birthplace of More.

In her early thirties Hannah became disillusioned with the theatrical world and, clearly searching for something, returned to Somerset and country life. Always a church attender, she now began to be influenced by the evangelicals who were shaking up the Church of England. Through encountering the converted slave trader John Newton, she experienced a conversion to a new and vibrant faith in Christ.

The Clapham Sect

Newton introduced her to William Wilberforce and their shared belief that the correct response to knowing Christ was to pursue right actions. Following them, Hannah became part of what was to be known as the 'Clapham Sect', a dynamic association of evangelicals with a vision to change Britain and the world for God, based around the then village of Clapham. The only woman involved, Hannah threw herself into their work, especially the writing of pamphlets, books and poems.

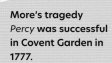

More's tragedy *Percy* **was successful in Covent Garden in 1777.**

Hannah became involved with the campaign against slavery. In 1788 she produced a powerful and widely read poem *Slavery* which condemned the practice. In it she wrote:

> ### What! does the immortal principle within
> ### Change with the casual colour of a skin?

Hannah's writings against the slave trade were widely circulated and had a significant impact in shifting public opinion towards its abolition.

In 1789 Wilberforce visited her, and encountering some of the local Somerset villages was appalled by their levels of poverty and ill health. He encouraged Hannah to become involved and with the help of her sisters she began various social initiatives, including

More devised *Cheap Repository Tracts* **to be sold or distributed to poor literate people.**

In 1802 More moved to Wrington, a village in the Mendip Hills, Somerset.

Sunday schools, day schools and other schemes to support the community. As these began to have an impact Hannah found herself accused of undermining the social order, a serious charge at a time when British society was in a panic over how the revolution in France had slid into anarchy and open atheism. Increasingly, Hannah and the 'Clapham activists' were forced to explain that they sought reformation rather than revolution.

Endlessly active, Hannah was also involved in the Bible Society, the Church Missionary Society, and animal welfare in setting up the organisation that became the RSPCA. She continued to publish books, pamphlets and a novel, all of which promoted evangelical Christianity and a commitment to those values of contentment, humility, work and family – characteristics of the Victorian period which began just after her death. Outliving sisters and colleagues Hannah continued to be productive, respected and widely consulted until she died in 1833 at the age of eighty-eight.

I think there are two elements about Hannah More's life that should not be overlooked.

• The first is her *conversion to Christ*. Well into her thirties, Hannah was a 'good person'; a respectable churchgoing individual of impeccable morality. Yet she came to realise that her faith was largely superficial and that she needed to experience that change of heart in which the living Christ took centre place in her life. One of my favourite quotations of hers is: 'There is one single fact which we may oppose to all the wit and argument of infidelity, namely, that no man ever repented of being a Christian on his death-bed.'

More's grave in the village of Wrington.

● A second element is the determined and energetic way in which Hannah expressed her new faith in her activism. As she wrote: 'Action is the life of virtue, and the world is the theatre of action.' Here three things stand out. I see that she had a *practical activism*. She was not simply a woman of words but someone who wanted to see things happen: laws passed, schools built, organisations founded. A challenge.

● I note, too, that hers was a *partnered activism*. Again as a writer, it might have been expected that she would work on her own. She didn't but instead showed enormous wisdom in working with others, whether with the enormously productive individuals of the 'Clapham Sect' or even those who were not believers. She built bridges, working with people rather than against them. Another challenge!

● Finally, I note that hers was a *persuasive activism*. When there's a cause to be fought there's always a temptation to go into a loud and aggressive mode. While it may be understandable it's often counter-productive. In contrast, Hannah, operating when women could not be involved in politics, quietly used her writing ability to popularise the causes she was passionate about. In doing so she warmed hearts with grace. To use a modern term, she was a subtle and effective 'influencer'. Yet another challenge!

I am challenged by Hannah More; let her challenge you too!

Title page of *Poems* by Hannah More.

G.K. CHESTERTON

One of the most important cultural figures a hundred years ago was G.K. Chesterton; an astonishingly prolific writer, speaker and defender of Christianity.

Gilbert Keith Chesterton was born in 1874 to a London family with a liberal religious faith, from which he soon drifted away. He studied art in London where he also took classes in literature, but left without any degree. Chesterton, intelligent and well read, began working in a publisher's offices but increasingly wrote art and literary criticism. His ability to rapidly produce appealing, thought-provoking articles on almost any topic was soon recognised and he began writing weekly columns for journals, something that continued for the rest of his life.

Chesterton's wife Frances, whom he married in 1901, was responsible for bringing him to faith in Christ. Increasingly, 'GKC' became a celebrated figure on the cultural landscape. In fluent and frequently humorous words he took a firm stand for a traditional Christianity and challenged many of the ideas of the early twentieth century. Chesterton became an imposing and popular speaker, debating with people such as George Bernard Shaw, H.G. Wells and Bertrand Russell. He was increasingly widely read and quoted, and in the 1930s began giving popular radio talks.

Campden Hill, Kensington (London),
where Chesterton was born.

Chesterton wrote a series of short stories featuring the crime-solving priest, *Father Brown*. The Cotswolds village of Blockley often features in the recent television series.

Chesterton died of heart failure at his home in Beaconsfield, Buckinghamshire on 14th June 1936 aged sixty-two.

A Prolific Author

Chesterton was remarkably prolific, somehow writing 80 books, several hundred poems, 200 short stories, 4,000 articles and several plays. He has been called 'a master without a masterpiece'. His three enduring achievements are his books defending Christianity, his poetry and his detective novels.

Alec Guinness starring as Father Brown (1954).

His two defences of the Christian faith – *Orthodoxy* and *The Everlasting Man* – have played a part in many conversions, including that of C.S. Lewis. In his poetry, Chesterton created some of the most memorable and popular poems of the English language. Perhaps Chesterton's most enduring achievement lies in his creation of Father Brown, an amateur detective who is a short, clumsy priest. In over fifty short stories, Father Brown succeeds in solving crimes, not because of his intelligence or deductive skills but – on the contrary – because he understands the depths of the human soul.

In his many writings Chesterton produced numerous quotable phrases, many of which involve some sort of paradox in which a truth is seen in a fresh and unexpected way. Let me give you some of my favourites:

'We do not want a Church that will move with the world. We want a Church that will move the world.'
G.K. CHESTERTON

G.K. CHESTERTON

George Bernard Shaw, Hilaire Belloc and G.K. Chesterton (L-R).

'These are the days when the Christian is expected to praise every creed except his own.'

'Fallacies do not cease to be fallacies because they become fashions.'

'The Christian ideal has not been tried and found wanting. It has been found difficult; and left untried.'

'The Bible tells us to love our neighbours, and also to love our enemies; probably because generally they are the same people.'

'Science must not impose any philosophy, any more than the telephone must tell us what to say.'

There is, too, the brilliantly brief response he wrote to a newspaper:

'Dear Sir: Regarding your article "What's Wrong with the World?" I am. Yours truly.'

Chesterton was a big man in every way. He got a lot right but even his greatest admirers admit he was flawed. So while he saw the threat of Hitler he was less critical of Mussolini; he had a naïve nostalgia for the Middle Ages and, perhaps most troubling today, wrote things that

Beaconsfield, Chesterton's home town for much of his life.

can be considered anti-Semitic. Nevertheless, as the Christian poet T.S. Eliot said, Chesterton 'was importantly and consistently on the side of the angels'.

As an evangelist I see Chesterton as one of the great defenders of the Christian faith in the twentieth century. He was resolutely, persistently and brilliantly countercultural, and in the wonderful way he spoke out I find three things worthy of praise.

A caricature of Chesterton by Max Beerbohm.

- First, Chesterton confronted his world with ***courage***. It was not easy being a traditional Christian in the early twentieth century when it was fashionable to have belief in progress and disbelief in religion. Undeterred, Chesterton boldly attacked atheism, agnosticism and liberal Christianity. He consistently reminded the people of God, Christ and their need for redemption.

- Second, Chesterton confronted his world with ***creativity***. He wrote an enormous amount on a variety of topics in many genres, but his Christian faith was there in everything. The result a multifaceted attack on unbelief: so, for example, those able to resist Chesterton's arguments in prose often found themselves challenged by his poetry.

- Finally, Chesterton confronted his world with ***charm***. All that he wrote bubbles with wit and humour. Although he battled against the most hostile of thinkers, he did so not with anger, but with generous grace. For all his zeal to confront, Chesterton made few enemies. In fact, the persistently happy tone of his writing may have had as much impact as the words themselves.

We could certainly benefit from having men and women like Chesterton today, who can defend the Christian faith with courage, creativity and charm.

> *'Do not be so open-minded that your brains fall out.'*
> **G.K. CHESTERTON**

ROSA PARKS

Some of my heroes are known for a lifetime of activity but some, like Rosa Parks, the woman whose quiet protest ended racial segregation in the United States, are known for what they did in a moment.

Rosa was born in Alabama in 1913 into an African-American community. When her parents separated she moved with her mother to a farm just outside the state capital, Montgomery. Although slavery had been abolished fifty years earlier, African-Americans suffered prejudice, abuse and intimidation, and were frequently subject to segregation.

Rosa's family were deeply involved in the church and had a profound faith. As Rosa later wrote, 'Prayer and the Bible became a part of my everyday thoughts and beliefs.' She remained involved in the church all her life, eventually becoming a deaconess.

In 1932 Rosa married Raymond Parks. He was active in the National Association for the Advancement of Colored People (NAACP), which defended the rights of African-Americans. In 1943 Rosa became active in the Civil Rights Movement where she worked as a secretary. As a priority was providing

Parks was born in Tuskegee, Alabama (USA).

legal help to those who had been deprived of justice, every day Rosa faced the appalling social inequality and frequent violence that black men and women encountered.

One focus of injustice centred on the buses. The city of Montgomery had a law that allowed the segregation of passengers by race and bus drivers commonly demanded that black passengers give up their seats when the 'whites only' seating was full.

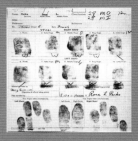

Parks' fingerprint card following her arrest on 1st December 1955.

On the evening of 1st December 1955 Rosa took the bus home and sat in an empty seat at the front of the section reserved for black people. As the 'whites only' section became full, the bus driver moved the 'colored' sign behind Rosa and three other people, and ordered them to give up their seats.

Courage

Three of them did but Rosa remained seated. When asked, 'Why don't you stand up?' she simply responded, 'I don't think I should have to stand up.' The driver said, 'Well, if you don't stand up, I'm going to have to call the police and have you arrested.' When writing about this moment later Rosa said,

Parks being fingerprinted following another arrest on 22nd February 1956.

'I instantly felt God give me the strength to endure whatever would happen next. God's peace flooded my soul, and my fear melted away.'

Her response was calm and dignified: 'You may do that.'

The bus that Parks was on when she refused to give up her seat, paving the way for the Montgomery Bus Boycott.

The police were called and Rosa was arrested and charged under the segregation law, found guilty and fined. However, by now support for her was gathering. The various organisations promoting African-American rights soon realised that this quiet, reputable forty-two-year-old woman was a suitable candidate to challenge the law. Courageously, she appealed against her conviction, challenging the very legality of racial segregation. She was backed by civil rights groups, churches and a financially damaging boycott of buses. Rosa's case went all the way to the United States Supreme Court where segregation was ruled unconstitutional.

Right Person, Right Time

Rosa found, as is so often the case, that victory came with a price. Both she and her husband lost their jobs and she became the subject of harassment and death threats. Despite becoming an honoured symbol of black dignity and strength, Rosa and her husband suffered financially. Raymond died in 1977 and Rosa died in 2005 at the age of ninety-two. In a remarkable final honour, the American government had her body lie in state in the U.S. Capitol.

You could say that Rosa became an 'accidental hero' but there is more than that. Rosa's action was not simply a random angry protest; there had been plenty of those and they achieved very little. This was where the right person did the right action in the right way at the right time.

Many women were arrested for violating an anti-boycott law.

There were three significant things in what Rosa Parks did.

- First, there was a ***godly preparation***. How any of us react in the spur of the moment is based on who we have become during our lifetime. In a sense, Rosa had been preparing for this confrontation all her life. Her personality and identity had been shaped by decades of Christian preaching, Bible study and prayer. The motto of the Boy Scouts is 'be prepared', guidance that could be applied to all of life. After all, none of us know when we are suddenly going to find ourselves in a crisis, faced with a difficult challenge to do what is right. Let's prepare ourselves in advance. Stay close to Christ and his word, let the Spirit mould who you are and you will be ready for whatever life throws against you.

U.S. President Obama sits on the bus that Parks was arrested on.

215

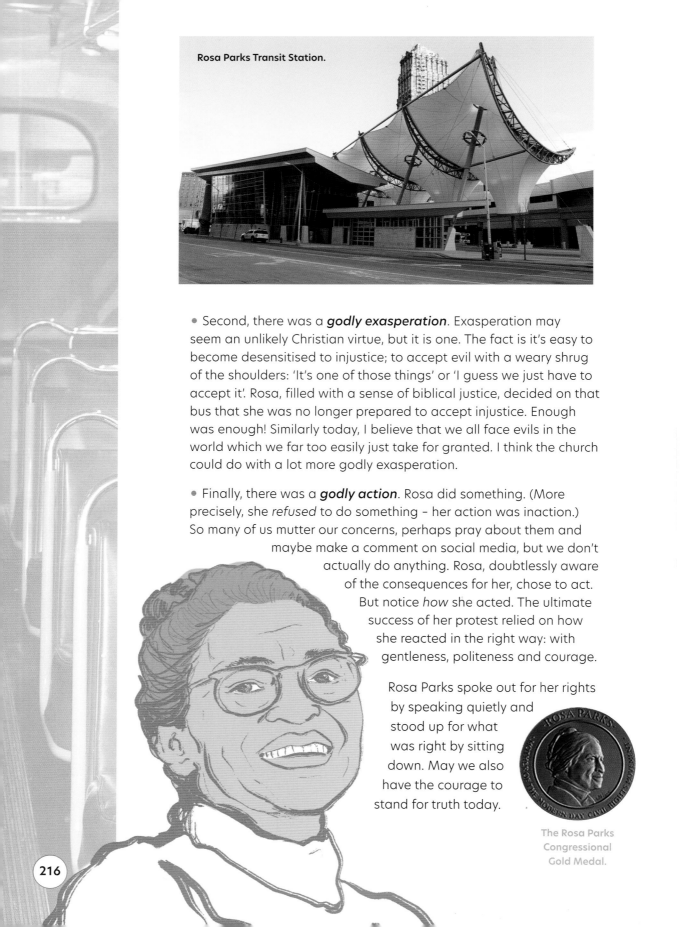

Rosa Parks Transit Station.

- Second, there was a **godly exasperation**. Exasperation may seem an unlikely Christian virtue, but it is one. The fact is it's easy to become desensitised to injustice; to accept evil with a weary shrug of the shoulders: 'It's one of those things' or 'I guess we just have to accept it'. Rosa, filled with a sense of biblical justice, decided on that bus that she was no longer prepared to accept injustice. Enough was enough! Similarly today, I believe that we all face evils in the world which we far too easily just take for granted. I think the church could do with a lot more godly exasperation.

- Finally, there was a **godly action**. Rosa did something. (More precisely, she *refused* to do something – her action was inaction.) So many of us mutter our concerns, perhaps pray about them and maybe make a comment on social media, but we don't actually do anything. Rosa, doubtlessly aware of the consequences for her, chose to act. But notice *how* she acted. The ultimate success of her protest relied on how she reacted in the right way: with gentleness, politeness and courage.

Rosa Parks spoke out for her rights by speaking quietly and stood up for what was right by sitting down. May we also have the courage to stand for truth today.

The Rosa Parks Congressional Gold Medal.

Picture Credits

p.50(T) The Apostolic Faith Mission, Azusa Street (1807). Public Domain.

p.52(T) Leaders of the Apostolic Faith Mission (image published in 1908). Public Domain.

p.54(B) Recruitment poster. Public Domain.

p.62(T) Amy Carmichael. Public Domain.

p.64(T) Published with kind permission of *The Dohnavur Fellowship* and *Friends of Dohnavur*.

p.66(T) Oil painting of Edward Jenner. Creative Commons (CC-BY-4.0): Wellcome Images, a website operated by Wellcome Trust.

p.66(B) The Chantry. Creative Commons (CC-BY-2.0). Attribution: Nick from Bristol.

p.67(M) 'Cuculus Canorus' published in *Natural History of the Birds of Central Europe*, 3rd Ed. by J.A. Naumann, revised by G. Berg et al. Edited by Carl R. Hennicke. Public Domain.

p.74(T) Mary Stone from *Women Workers of the Orient* by Margaret Ernestine Burton (Central Committee on the United Study of Foreign Missions, 1918). Public Domain.

p.86(L), p.88(L), p.89(B) Bach's manuscript of the Sonata for Violin Solo No.1 in G Minor (BWV 1001). Public Domain.

p.90(B) Magdalene College, Cambridge. Creative Commons (CC-BY-SA-2.0). Photograph © Andrew Dunn, November 2004.

p.94(B) Earlham Hall. Creative Commons (CC-BY-SA-2.0). Photograph © George Littleboy, June 2006.

p.98(B) *The Night Watch* by Rembrandt. Public Domain.

p.99(T) *The Artist in His Studio* by Rembrandt. Public Domain.

p.99(B) The Rembrandt House Museum. Creative Commons (CC-BY-SA-2.5). Attribution: Voytikof.

p.100(T) Rembrandt House Museum. Creative Commons (CC-BY-SA-3.0). Attribution: Johnbod

p.100(B) Self-portrait by Rembrandt. Public Domain.

p.101(T) *Return of the Prodigal Son* by Rembrandt. Public Domain.

p.102(T) Revd Dr John R.W. Stott. Creative Commons (CC-BY-3.0). Photo owned by Langham Partnership International.

p.106(L), p.108(L) Engraving of Spurgeon preaching at the Music Hall, Royal Surrey Gardens (Sheldon & Co., 1858). Public Domain.

p.110(T) Lilias Trotter (c. 1888). Public Domain.

p.112(T) Scenes of North Africa by Lilias Trotter © Lilias Trotter Legacy.

p.113(T) Portrait of John Ruskin by Lilias Trotter © Lilias Trotter Legacy.

p.114(L), p.116(L), p117(M) The Faraday Disk published in *The Electric Light: Its History, Production, and Applications* by Émile Alglave and J. Boulard, translated by T. O'Conor Sloan (D. Appleton & Co., New York, 1884). Public Domain.

p.116(T) Watercolour of Michael Faraday's study at the Royal Institution by Harriet Jane Moore (c. 1850). Public Domain.

p.118(L), p.121(B) *Arachis hypogaea* in *Köhler's Medizinal-Pflanzen* by Franz Eugen Köhler (1887). Public Domain.

p.118(B) Photographic portrait of George Washington Carver by F.B. Johnston (c. 1906). Library of Congress Prints and Photographs Division Washington, D.C. 20540, USA. Image restored by Adam Cuerden. Public Domain.

p.119(T) Photograph of George Washington Carver standing in a field by F.B. Johnston (c. 1906). Library of Congress Prints and Photographs Division Washington, D.C. 20540, USA. Public Domain.

p.120(T) Peanut specimen collected by Carver. Public Domain.

p.122(T) Gladys Aylward in China. Public Domain.

p.130(T) Portrait of James Clerk Maxwell. Cavendish Laboratory, University of Cambridge. Public Domain.

p.130(B) James Clerk Maxwell's birthplace. Creative Commons (CC-BY-SA-4.0) Attribution: Stephen C. Dickson.

p.130(L), p.132(L) The rings of Saturn. NASA/JPL. Public Domain.

p.131(M) The rings of Saturn. NASA, ESA and E. Karkoschka (University of Arizona). Public Domain.

p.134(T) Self-portrait by William Holman Hunt (1867). Public Domain.

p.142(T) Amanda Smith (c. 1899). Public Domain.

p.142(L), p.143(B), p.144(L) Camp Meeting of the Methodists in N. America (c. 1819) by J.G. Milbert. Library of Congress Prints and Photographs Division Washington, D.C. 20540, USA. Public Domain.

p.149(T) Watercolour of HMS Fly (c. 1848) by Richard Aldworth Oliver. Public Domain,

p.150(L), p.152(L), p.153(T) *Psychology: Stri Dharma Niti* by Pandita Ramabai (Kolkata, 1882). Public Domain.

p.151(B) Pandita Ramabai and her daughter in 'The Work of the Pandita Ramabai' by Saint Nihal Singh, *Southern Workman* (October 1911). Public Domain.

p.152(T) Pandita Ramabai's Mukti Home at dinner, Dodballapur (October 1906), Council for World Mission Archive, SOAS Library.

p.154(B) Kingston Square and 'Drainside' in *Hudson Taylor In Early Years: The Growth of a Soul* by Dr and Mrs Howard Taylor (Morgan and Scott, 1911). Public Domain.

p.156(T) The Lammermuir Party of Missionaries in *The Jubilee Story of the China Inland Mission* by Marshall Broomhall (London: Morgan and Scott, 1915). Public Domain.

p.159(L), p.160(L), p.162(L) Photograph of Sistine Chapel ceiling. Creative Commons (CC-BY-SA-3.0). Attribution: Qypchak.

p.159(T) Photograph with kind permission from the family.

p.160(B) Photograph with kind permission from the family.

p.164(L), p.166(L), p.168(L), p.168(T) Drawing of the slave deck of the Marie Séraphique by René Lhermitte (1770). Public Domain.

p.164(B) *Slave Traffic* by S. Hutchinson (1793). Public Domain.

p.165(M) Iron foot rings for prisoners. Creative Commons (CC-BY-SA-4.0). Attribution: wereldculturen.nl

p.167(T) *Olney Hymns*, published by John Newton and William Cowper in 1779. Pubic Domain.

p.174(L), p.176(L), p.178(L), p.178(B) *In Darkest England and the Way Out*, Salvation Army Social Campaign (1890). Public Domain.

p.175(T) Manifesto of The Salvation Army (1878). Public Domain.

p.184(T) Synodal elections 1933. Creative Commons. Attribution: Gregor Helms. Public Domain.

p.188(B) Crosby's birthplace in *Memories Of Eighty Years* (Boston: James H. Earle & Co., 1906).

p.190(T) Crosby and Van Alstyne in Fanny Crosby's Life-Story, ed. Will Carleton (New York, NY: Every Where Publishing, 1903).

p.190(B) Front cover of *Fanny Crosby's Life-Story*, ed. Will Carleton (New York, NY: Every Where Publishing, 1903).

p.192(T) St Francis. Public Domain.

p.192(B) St Francis' birthploce. Creative Commons (CC-BY-SA-3.0). Attribution: Tetraktys.

p.200(T) Photograph with kind permission from the family.

p.204(B) Birthplace of More. Creative Commons (CC-BY-SA-3.0). Attribution: Robert Powell.

p.204(L), p.206(L), p.207(B) Title page of *Poems* by Hannah More (1816). Public Domain.

p.205(T) The Theatre Royal, Covent Garden, engraving published as Plate 100 of *Microcosm of London* (1810). Public Domain.

p.205(B) Cheap Repository tract by Hannah More (1817). Creative Commons (CC-BY-SA-4.0). Attribution: Das48.

p.208(L), p.210(L), p.211(T) Caricature of G.K. Chesterton by Max Beerbohm in *English Humorists of Today* by J.A. Hammerton (London: Hodder and Stoughton, 1907).

p.212(T) Rosa Parks (1955). National Archives and Records Administration Records of the U.S. Information Agency. Record Group 306.

p.213(T) Rosa Parks' fingerprint card (1955). National Archives and Records Administration: Southeast Region, East Point, GA.

p.213(M) Rosa Parks being fingerprinted. Associated Press 1956. Public Domain. Photograph restored by Adam Cuerden.

p.214(T) Photograph of the Rosa Parks bus. Creative Commons (CC-BY-SA-3.0). Attribution: Rmhermen.

p.216(T) Rosa Parks Transit Center. Creative Commons (CC-BY-SA-3.0). Atrribution: Dwight Burdette.

p.216(B) Rosa Parks Congressional Gold Medal designed by Artis Lane. Public Domain.